D1522629

Meryl Streep

Meryl Streep
A Critical Biography

by
Eugene E. Pfaff, Jr.
and
Mark Emerson

LIBRARY
SEMINOLE COMMUNITY COLLEGE

REC. OCT 1 2 1988

SANFORD, FLORIDA
32771

McFarland & Company, Inc., Publishers
Jefferson, North Carolina, and London

Library of Congress Cataloguing-in-Publication Data

Pfaff, Eugene E., 1948–
 Meryl Streep : a critical biography.

 Bibliography: p. 139.
 Filmography: p. 127.
 1. Streep, Meryl. 2. Actors—United States—
Biography. I. Emerson, Mark. II. Title.
PN2287.S78P45   1987   792'.028'0924 [B]   87-22636

ISBN 0-89950-287-3 (acid-free natural paper)

© 1987 Eugene E. Pfaff and Martin L. Hester, Jr.

All rights reserved.

Printed in the United States of America.

McFarland   Box 611   Jefferson NC 28640

To my father and the memory of my mother.
— E.E.P.

To my mother, and to the memory of my father.
— M.E.

Table of Contents

Acknowledgments

The authors are particularly indebted to Raymond Strait, whose generous advice and assistance proved invaluable in writing this book. We also thank our families for their patience during many long months. Mr. Pfaff also expresses appreciation to his father, Eugene E. Pfaff, Sr., for his example of what good writing and meticulous scholarship are all about.

1
Images

The hostile audience stares at Joanna Kramer as she sits in the witness stand. Having abandoned her husband and six-year-old son eighteen months before, she now has returned to claim custody of the boy from the father who sacrificed his career and restructured his life around his son.

Joanna sits with hands folded in her lap, striving to control her emotions as she contemplates her hopeless situation. She is radiantly beautiful: golden hair pulled back from high cheekbones and blue, cerebral eyes.

She begins to speak in a soft, almost inaudible voice. Avoiding histrionics, yet crying in spite of herself, she painfully sheds away layer after layer of her past. What emerges is a woman who has been trapped in a suffocating marriage to an insensitive advertising agent. Ted Kramer is so obsessed with his career that he cannot recognize how he is stifling Joanna's own search for identity and self-esteem. Through her testimony, Joanna slowly reveals herself to be a woman so unhappy that she cannot even care for her own child any longer.

Under cross-examination, her face dissolves from one contradictory emotion to another in a disturbing succession of guilt and self-doubt that begins to crumble her facade of cool composure, her eyes conveying the depth of anguish at having abandoned her child.

It is a devastating performance that not only rocks the audience, but her husband, Ted, as he comes to understand Joanna's agony. As Ted and Joanna exchange frightened stares at what their lives have become, each comes to understand the torment of the other. In that defenseless moment, the audience takes Joanna to their hearts. By her sensitive, moving testimony, Meryl Streep has accomplished the all-but-impossible task of changing the audience's perception of Joanna from one of hostility to sympathetic understanding.

The magazine reporter is disconcerted; the interview is not at all as she had expected.

Meryl Streep, the mother who abandoned her child in *Kramer vs. Kramer*, is the epitome of adoring motherhood as she sits on the couch with her six-week-old daughter. The actress who has won acclaim for her role involving domestic strife speaks glowingly of a marriage that combines traditional ideas of love and commitment with contemporary notions of male-female equality.

The hottest actress in Hollywood has placed her highly successful career on hold to spend time with her family. Interrupting a brilliant career just as it is reaping the rewards of stardom is not the typical Hollywood scenario, but the reporter quickly grasps that Meryl Streep is not the typical movie star.

Wandering about the simply furnished apartment in Manhattan's Lower East Side, she notices the absence of memorabilia from Streep's stage and screen career. There are no pictures of Meryl with celebrities and dignitaries. Two Oscars and an Emmy lie almost hidden among the papers that clutter her desk; there is no evidence at all that she is the most highly acclaimed actress of her generation.

The aloof, pristine beauty of *The French Lieutenant's Woman* and *Sophie's Choice* laughs frequently, punctuates her conversation with an occasionally earthy remark, and performs pratfalls for the photographer. Just as suddenly, she leans forward, speaking intently about her profession.

The reporter, like so many others, is impressed with this complex, enigmatic superstar who has rejected the "star system" and successfully separated the private woman from the public figure.

The cloaked and motionless figure of a woman stands on the windswept breakwater, staring out at the churning gray sea.

A tall Victorian gentleman, concerned for her safety, leaves the side of his fiancee and struggles over the spray-lashed stones, his shouts of warning lost in the rising wind. As he approaches her, the mysterious figure turns, plucks aside the rough cloth of her hood and stares at him, then returns to her silent vigil.

He is transfixed by the haunted look of her pale, delicate beauty. But it is not the shrouded figure, not the beauty that so troubles him; it is from the look of utter desolation and torment in her eyes that he retreats in confused distraction. There is something alarming in that tragic, unforgettable face, with its sorrowful eyes that reveal the despair within her soul.

This scene so rivets the audience that they share the man's discomfort and, like him, are irresistibly drawn to the mysterious woman. The intense scene is one of the film's most dramatic moments.

Meryl Streep emerges from the subway exit at Fifty-seventh and Third Avenue in New York and glances momentarily at her picture on the cover of a magazine at a nearby coffee counter.

She casually window-shops up Fifty-seventh Street before entering Bloomingdale's. With sunglasses perched on top of her head, hair pulled back loosely into a bun, jeans, blue running shoes and a jade-green turtleneck sweater, she is indistinguishable from thousands of other shoppers. Despite this anonymity, a man approaches her.

"Did anyone ever tell you that you look exactly like Meryl what's-her-name?" he asks.

"No, nobody ever did," replies Meryl. "But thanks anyway."

Late that afternoon, she returns to the subway. As she approaches the train, she glances down to see the magazine with her picture on the cover crumpled and dirty on the platform. She flings back her head and laughs at the transience of fame.

With tears welling in her eyes, Sophie Zawistowska, in a rare moment of honesty, strips away the tapestry of lies that has become her life and bares her soul to her ardent admirer, Stingo.

"The truth?" she mutters huskily. "What is the truth? After all the lies that I have told."

The audience focuses on that gentle, beautiful face as Sophie reveals the dark secret she has carried deep within her for so many years. The soft contralto voice, with its heavy Polish accent, speaks in somber tones of dehumanized existence in a Nazi concentration camp. It is a story that weaves an engrossing spell over the audience.

The emotional toll of Sophie's catastrophic past is clearly evident. She nervously twists a strand of hair between her fingers. Her eyes cast furtive glances around the room. Sophie's speech comes in halting starts and stops.

As Sophie, Meryl Streep meticulously strips away the stratagems and deceptions by which she has avoided confronting her past. As she does so, the audience perceives the real Sophie: guilt-ridden and emotionally fragmented. It is an extraordinary, heart-breaking performance in which Sophie emerges as fine and beautiful—and ultimately doomed.

Sophie and her lover, Nathan, lie on the bed, arms intertwined in death. The camera lingers on Sophie's pale, delicately beautiful face, then pans back slowly from the two tragic lovers.

"Cut. Print," shouts director Alan Pakula. The room erupts into frenzied activity as the makeup crew and lighting technicians rush to set up the next scene.

Kevin Kline smiles broadly, making a joke to his co-star, Meryl Streep, who rises, oblivious to the chaos swirling around her. The death scene in *Sophie's Choice* forces the painful memory of another deathbed—not in the fantasized world of a sound studio, but the grim reality of a hospital intensive care unit.

John Cazale lies on the bed, tubes running into his nose and mouth, his forehead beaded with perspiration from his labored breathing. Beside him, Meryl Streep whispers words of comfort that she knows he cannot hear.

For the last nine months, she has neglected her career to devote herself to John, keeping his spirits up and never losing the hope he would defeat the disease that was ravaging his body. But now the last of her hopes fades with each shallow breath that John's pain-racked body takes.

These final, tortured hours of John's battle against cancer are the end of their two-year love affair. As Meryl tightly grips his hand, her mind struggles against the numbness of grief, trying to cope with the first tragedy of her Cinderella life.

These diverse public and private images reflect the complexity of one of the most intelligent and exciting actresses of our age: Meryl Streep.

She is the hottest young actress in Hollywood, and publicity is raging around her. Her picture has appeared on the cover of *Time*, *Newsweek*, *Life*, and *Rolling Stone*; scores of magazines tout her as "the finest actress of her generation" and "the Woman of the '80s." Film critics have exhausted the range of superlatives in describing her talent. Studio producers mention her name for every female role. Hollywood's leading actors vie to co-star with her. She is nominated for an Oscar year after year.

Her life does not simmer with scandal of drug addiction or alcoholism, or torrid love affairs. Yet women are drawn to her and men find her sensual and alluring. What is it about Meryl Streep that generates such lavish praise and attention?

In a society jaded by the sensational excesses of celebrity lifestyles, Meryl is refreshingly unpretentious. She symbolizes the problems of contemporary women striving to successfully combine a career and family life. In such diverse films as *Kramer vs. Kramer*, *The French Lieutenant's Woman*, *Sophie's Choice* and *Silkwood*, she has given unparalleled dimension to women's roles, extending them beyond stereotypes into intricate, sensitive performances. Most of all, Meryl has brought back a glamour, talent and elegance to the screen that has been absent in recent years.

How does Meryl Streep create the uniquely indelible screen images that have Hollywood's top producers, directors and actors clamoring for her?

It is a subtle, elusive talent that directors simply call "the Streep Syndrome." Her acting exudes a mystery, an arresting combination of vulnerability and strength. In vivid, compelling performances, she conveys the inner crises of the characters she portrays. She has the ability to make them seem real people with whom the audience can identify. "It's like painting a portrait," she once told a reporter. "When it comes off, it's a thrill."[1]

To millions of moviegoers it is more simple: she is sexy, sassy and smart. She is something new and exciting among recent American actresses: an independent woman who combines sensual beauty and high intelligence.

Meryl is an exotic newcomer to Hollywood, one whose face and mannerisms have influenced a generation, much like Jean Harlow in the 1930s, Marilyn Monroe in the 1950s and Jane Fonda in the 1970s. Her talent has been compared to such screen legends as Bette Davis and Katherine Hepburn, and her allure to that of Ingrid Bergman, Liv Ullman and Greta Garbo. But she is a unique talent who brings intuitive authenticity and originality to each role.

Film critics have different theories as to what has made Meryl Streep such a brilliant new star. One might say it is her beauty: 5′6″, serene blue eyes, ash-blonde hair, lustrous skin, high cheekbones and a figure as delicate as a tapered candle. She has the classical features from a more romantic era.

Another critic might argue that it is more than just beauty, pointing out the mannerisms that bring memorable, subtle nuances to her characters. Fluttering hands, facial gestures and head twitches dot her contained, yet moving performances. She adapts her flexible face to the character she is portraying. Contrasting emotions play subtly across her features, from wanton allure to fragile vulnerability. Her voice ranges from soft and mellow to shrill and raucous.

Still other reviewers cite her uncanny instinct for the impromptu, the precise movement or gesture which seems so natural and inevitable; through these movements, she registers a remarkable range of looks and gestures. The diverse qualities of Meryl Streep add up to a single word: superstar.

But beneath the superstar image lies a complex human being. There are many Meryl Streeps, and none of them conforms to the typical Hollywood movie-star image. She is as enigmatic as the ambiguous heroines she portrays on screen. Showered with praise and publicity, she has rejected the glamour of Hollywood and the trappings of stardom. Absent are the luxurious mansion and the fawning entourage. She and her husband, Don Gummer, live quietly in rural east Connecticut, shunning publicity. She guards her privacy so intensely that she will not allow any photographs of her home or her three children.

But she is no spoiled prima donna. Unlike the aloof women she portrays, she is unassuming, yet articulate in discussing the techniques of her profession. Strength of character and a realistic sense of her own worth have enabled Meryl to pursue a career on her own terms, refusing to be typecast. Her malleable features and remarkably versatile talent have allowed her to play an extraordinary range of parts from leading ladies to aged hags, from Shakespeare to knockabout farce. Although her classic looks could have enabled her to play an endless succession of vacuous "blonde" roles, she has chosen instead to test her range by a diversity of challenging parts, taking chances with her career by portraying unpleasant and unattractive character roles.

But can she maintain this independence as pressures mount with her career? Studio heads find a particular quality and attempt to exploit it. Hollywood has historically punished mavericks like Meryl Streep and enforced conformity. Meryl is aware of the inherent jealousy of overnight successes, the fickle idolatry of fans and the transient enthusiasm of movie producers. But her talent, versatility and an intense professional commitment have enabled her to resist typecasting. Hollywood moneymen have seen her ability to portray a diverse range of roles. Even more, they are impressed with the box-office success of her films and the consistency with which she receives Oscar nominations.

Meryl remains secure in her own sense of values and identity. Brilliant and outspoken, she is not afraid to take risks or accept professional challenges.

2
In the Beginning

Meryl Streep is currently riding a wave of popularity following her 1980 and 1982 Oscars. As the most sought-after actress in Hollywood, she enjoys the leverage of a bankable star whose stature ensures a million dollars a picture and influence over casting and script decisions. Although her career has been meteoric, Meryl has worked undeniably hard to achieve her phenomenal success. She has paid her dues by honing and perfecting her talent through the rigors of the New York stage.

She has entered a crucial phase of her career, where the pressures and pitfalls of stardom are gathering around her. One such pressure is to ride the crest of the wave by accepting as many roles as possible for maximum public exposure. But Meryl refused to lend her name or talent to mediocre films; she has carefully chosen her roles, determined to maintain the high quality of films she has done so far.

Then there are her strong—and outspoken—feelings about the stereotypical roles for women in films. Despite her turning down such sex-ploitative potboilers as Sidney Sheldon's *Bloodlines* and *Scruples*, she is not averse to films with explicit sex scenes. She was interested in *The Postman Always Rings Twice*, but insisted that co-star Jack Nicholson be equally explicit. In the end, the producers gave the part to Jessica Lange.[1]

With her classical beauty and a figure that is the envy of other actresses, she could easily become the sex symbol of the eighties. But she is a shrewd analyst of the transient nature of such roles, and remains ambivalent about her beauty, which is not the predominant reason for her success. She has been described as being "among a new breed of classically trained New York–based actresses . . . whose career is distinctly 'non–Hollywood' and only marginally based on looks."[2] Free from the constraints of "glamour," she possesses a unique combination of elegance and earthiness, and a versatility that allows her to play virtually any role.

Another pressure stems from her political activism, ranging from women's rights to nuclear disarmament. Although she is aware of the possible risks to her career, she continues to appear as a speaker at antinuclear rallies and lends her support to numerous other causes.

Despite these pressures, Meryl has pursued her career with a fierce independence and creative energy that has earned her the nickname "the female Laurence Olivier." Although casual in her personal life, she is a tenacious perfectionist in her professional one. She made it clear from the beginning of her career that she was aiming for the top and could accept nothing less than the best from herself and her colleagues. Meryl readily admits to being almost obsessive about the quality of her work. "What I have is more like *over*drive. Success doesn't feel like success. I apply myself to each role with the same commitment. I don't do junk."[3]

Her choice of roles reveals this intense commitment to her profession and her breadth as an actress. She first attracted the attention of film critics and audiences in *The Deer Hunter*, in which she portrayed Linda, an all–American girl waiting for her man to come home from the Vietnam War. Next was the phenomenal role of Joanna Kramer in *Kramer vs. Kramer*, where she sensitively played the warring emotions of anguish, despair, and determination within a woman involved in a wrenching child custody suit. Following that was *The French Lieutenant's Woman*, involving the distraught, tragic heroine who voluntarily makes a social outcast of herself after being jilted by her lover. After that was the brilliant *Sophie's Choice*, her Oscar-winning portrayal of a woman doomed by her sense of guilt and grief. *Silkwood* is a stunning performance of a strong, defiant union activist. Each of these characters draws upon different facets of Meryl Streep's extraordinary acting ability, and none of them confines her to the "suffering madonna" ingenues predicted for her by critics at the beginning of her career.

Her career has about it the mythical quality of a Hollywood overnight success story. In less than a decade, she has won an Obie, an Emmy and two Oscars. For her role in *Kramer vs. Kramer*, she was paid $300,000, a real bargain in view of the millions that the film made at the box office. But times have changed; her salary for *Silkwood* was over twice that, with future roles commanding a cool $1,000,000. Not bad for an actress who made her screen debut in 1977.

How has Meryl Streep made it so big, so fast?

She was not the kind of a child one would think destined for superstardom. She was born Mary Louise Streep on April 22, 1949, in Summit, New Jersey, the eldest child and only daughter of Henry and Mary Streep. Within months, her mother had contracted the awkward double name to a more manageable Meryl; besides, it went better with her Dutch surname.

Henry Streep was a successful executive in the prestigious pharmaceutical firm of Merck, Inc., and Mary was an independent commercial artist who worked at home. Within a year, they had moved to Bernardsville, New Jersey, an affluent, upwardly mobile, middle-class suburb in the center of the state. A pleasant little village of one-story frame and brick buildings, open and green, it boasted a population of only 4000. In 1951, Henry III (called Third) was born, followed by Dana in 1953.

The Streeps were a close, loving family, and Henry and Mary doted on their three children, constantly taking them into New York City to the theater, ballet and ball games. It would seem an idyllic life for a little girl.

But Meryl remembers her childhood as an agonizing period of self-doubt and self-loathing. Humiliated by her glasses, permed hair, fat cheeks and braces, she unleased her frustration on all around her, becoming a virtual tyrant over her younger brothers. "She was a bit of a terror," says Third, "and pretty ghastly."[4]

In her fantasies, Meryl wanted to be liked by her classmates; in reality, she was so moody and introverted that she was quickly ostracized. "Nobody liked me," she recalls. "I was bossy, prim and determined."[5]

Things got so bad that one day the other children chased her home from school, taunting her. She had to climb a tree to escape, while they hit her legs with sticks.

Meryl lived in this private hell of insecurity and humiliation throughout elementary school. In her misery, she became a prematurely somber child-adult with a bossy nature and a fiery temper.

Longing for attention, at twelve she found solace in her one asset: a delicate contralto voice. She stunned the audience with a beautiful solo French rendition of *O Holy Night* during the school Christmas play. Her parents believed that she had a promising voice worth training and immediately enrolled her in voice lessons under the renowned Estelle Liebling in New York. It was several years before Meryl discovered that the "nice lady" who had the lesson ahead of her was opera diva Beverly Sills.

At Bernards High School, Meryl began what she later called "my first characterization." Tired of her homely looks and determined to enjoy her high school years, she underwent a radical transformation to become a magazine-cover knockout: She replaced her thick glasses with contacts, peroxided her hair and removed her braces.

The transformation was nothing less than miraculous; suddenly, the morose, plain-Jane misfit had bloomed into a radiantly beautiful teenager. All of the Cinderella dreams of her lonely childhood came true with dazzling success. She became a cheerleader, dated football players, was named to the honor society, joined the swim team and was elected Homecoming Queen her senior year. It all seemed like the plot of a teenage romance novel.

Ironically, the realization of her dreams did not make Meryl happy. She quickly became dissatisfied with the shallowness of high school popularity status. "I thought that if I looked pretty and had all of the 'right things,' everyone would like me," she once reflected. "But . . . it made me terribly unhappy. My biggest decision every day used to be what clothes I should wear to school. It was ridiculous."[6] Instead of feeling accepted and popular, she felt like a role-playing outsider. She began to look for something else.

That "something else" proved to be drama. Her social activities had caused her to end her weekly voice lessons at fifteen, but those three years of training enabled her to win the role of Marian the Librarian in the junior class play, *The Music Man*. She had no theatrical ambitions; in fact, it took several days for her to muster the courage to audition. But she was a hit, and through that experience she discovered her dramatic flair. "If I can locate the moment when I was first bitten, that was it. The whole audience stood up when I came out. I've never had that experience since."[7]

Finally, the shy recluse, who so ached to be accepted and admired, had found something of value that satisfied her. Meryl came alive on stage. To her, acting was "just fun," but to several faculty members it was a window to an enormous talent. Her senior English teacher, Jean Galbraith, dropped in on rehearsals and heard her sing "Till There Was You" like a professional; she was amazed that it could be the same demure girl who sat in the front row staring out of the window. Drama teacher Dick Everhart was even more impressed: "When she walked out on the stage there was nobody else there."[8]

But Meryl paid a price for finding her niche. There was a growing sense of jealousy among the other girls as Meryl went on to capture the leads in *L'il Abner* and *Oklahoma!* Meryl accepted their animosity with the stubborn determination that has made her the outstanding actress of her generation; if that was the price that she must pay, so be it. A spark had been kindled deep within her and no one could take it from her.

Apart from drama, very little else interested Meryl in high school. She made good grades, but became a student who was good at anything and serious about nothing. "I wasn't really popular," Meryl remembers. "I tried to get good grades and be like the girls in the magazines. I spent a lot of time with my clothes, my hairdos and all that stuff because I thought it had something to do with the kind of person I was. It didn't, really, but I didn't realize that until I went away to college."[9]

Vassar is one of the elite Ivy League "Seven Sister" colleges for affluent and intellectually gifted young American women. There was never any question in Meryl's mind that she would go there. To Henry Streep, that was enough; he would see to it. As in childhood, Meryl was enjoying all of the comfortable advantages that intellect, money and privilege could provide.

But Meryl was becoming dissatisfied with the conformity of her high school years; she began to reject the placid "beauty queen" image with the same tenacity with which she had created it. In fact, her fiercely independent nature almost prevented her from entering Vassar. Henry accompanied her in the late summer to the final interview before the beginning of the fall semester. Enjoying the heady post-graduate freedom, Meryl had spent the summer on a local swim team. When the interviewer asked her what books she read that summer, Meryl panicked. Her reading had been limited to one book, albeit an impressive one: Carl Jung's *Modern Man in Search of a Soul.* She nervously mentioned it, pronouncing Jung's name with a hard "J." Fixing Meryl with a cold stare, the interviewer corrected her mispronunciation.

Meryl flushed with anger and rose from her seat. "Daddy, take me home," she said to the startled Henry. Ruffled feelings were quickly soothed, and she entered Vassar in the fall of 1967. But Meryl never forgot the incident. Years later, she would recall her anger: "That was the biggest book anybody ever read over any summer, and she was yelling at me because I didn't say the name right!"[10]

Despite this awkward beginning, Meryl found Vassar to be a liberating experience. The late 1960s was a period of turmoil and confusion for thousands of college students confronting rapid social change: mass rallies protesting the war in Vietnam, Black Nationalism, feminists calling attention to women's rights and the hard rock and drugs of the "turn on, tune in, drop out" generation.

But Meryl was lukewarm to most of the late sixties furor. She was as opposed to the Vietnam War as any of the other students, but was turned off by the hypocrisy she saw in the antiwar movement on the Vassar campus. It was the first year that Vassar had accepted male coeds, and the forty-two males quickly seized center stage in campus agitation among the 1600 women. "The whole strike committee was boys," she remembered later. "They took over and got off on it. These boys would get up and perform. Everybody was a mini–Abbie Hoffman in front of this adoring swarm of girls."[11]

Turned off by the campus activists, Meryl focused attention upon herself in anguished self-examination. The Homecoming Queen role had haunted her all through high school and she longed to divest herself of it. High school had been a suffocating, conformist society. Now, among bright young women from all over the country, she yearned to seek out her own identity as a person and a woman without role-playing. But would people like her for herself, or only if she conformed to an artificial role? She was determined to put her fears about the reasons for her popularity to the test at Vassar.

She dropped the Homecoming Queen role and began to wear the accoutrements of the counterculture: jeans, an old felt hat, black turtleneck sweater and boots. She deliberately did things to shock her friends, such as going as long as two months without washing her hair and performing feverish marathon Turkish dances in the dorm during closed study hours. To her amazement, although she gave everyone ample opportunity to dismiss her as an eccentric "freak," she found that she was readily accepted and made friends quickly.[12]

Now she could begin a search for her true identity, the "real" Meryl Streep, without her incessant anxieties. A real personality began to emerge. "Suddenly I felt accepted by the entire other half of the human race," she recalls. "From the time I entered college . . . I never felt the need to compete with anyone. That just all went out the window." She attended seminars that stretched her considerable intellectual talents and broadened her perspectives. "At Vassar, it was commonplace to give your best shot, so that became a habit. I learned to believe in myself. I acquired a genuine sense of identity."[13]

While enjoying the intellectual opportunities and newfound freedom at Vassar, Meryl still had not found any direction to her studies or serious thoughts as to her future; by her junior year, she still had not declared a major. Remembering how she had enjoyed drama at Bernards, she signed up for Introduction to Drama under instructor Clinton Atkinson. One day he asked her to read the passage from *Streetcar Named Desire* in which Blanche DuBois is taken to a mental hospital after suffering a complete nervous breakdown. Atkinson immediately recognized her talent. "Her acting was hair-raising, absolutely mindboggling," he would tell reporters later. "I don't think anyone ever taught Meryl acting; she really taught herself."[14]

After class, Atkinson asked her to read for the upcoming campus production of August Strindberg's *Miss Julie*. Embarrassed, Meryl agreed to attend that evening's audition. Ernest Springhern, head of Vassar's drama department, was in the audience that evening as Meryl nervously began to read. "After about ten minutes, I saw that Meryl was just outstanding. It hit you right in the eye." He looked across the small auditorium at Atkinson and silently nodded.[15]

Meryl was stunned when Atkinson offered her the lead; she had been hoping for one of the two lesser roles. Involving only three characters, *Miss Julie* is a very complex play, difficult for even seasoned professionals; with only three musical performances in high school, Meryl had won the most difficult role in her first audition. The part was that of a sexually decadent aristocrat, which Meryl played superbly. "She was a brilliant actress," says Atkinson. "She played Miss Julie with a voluptuousness that was almost shocking in someone her age."[16]

Impressed with her natural acting ability, Atkinson regularly cast her in ensuing productions. Meryl quickly became *the* star of the Vassar drama department. Atkinson could see that Meryl had the talent to go beyond college theater; he wanted to expose her to professional theater as a career. During the spring break, he invited her to accompany him to New York during the spring vacation, where he directed her in the off–Broadway production of *The Playboy of Seville* at the Cubiculo Theater.

That experience ignited a burning desire that had long smouldered deep within Meryl. Drama now became a passionate obsession. In her senior year, she participated in an exchange program at Dartmouth College, where she spent a semester heavily laden with dramatic arts courses.

She declared her major in drama and concentrated in costume design, playwriting and the dance. By the time of her graduation from Vassar in the spring of 1971, Meryl had finally made the commitment she had been seeking so desperately. Now she would become an actress.

After graduation, she took Atkinson's advice and decided to test her newfound commitment in summer stock. After all, she had only appeared in amateur college productions; if she was serious about her career choice, she should see what professional acting was all about and test her talents against more demanding audiences.

Meryl worked that summer with the Green Mountain Guild, a summer repertory company in Woodstock, Vermont. She found the experience exhilarating and decided to remain with the company throughout that fall and winter. They performed short pieces by Shaw and Chekhov in school auditoriums and local ski resorts.

Repertory theater requires an intense commitment both to one's art and fellow actors; it demands a grueling schedule which tolerates no prima donnas. One must be willing to be a set designer, jack-leg carpenter, seamstress, scriptwriter, go-fer, typist and—last, but not least—an actor. To those that survive, it can be the most rewarding, purest theater an actor ever performs, and create bonds that go deeper than mere friendships.

The daily challenge of repertory was Meryl's metier, and she thrived on it. Meryl later summed up that summer fondly: "We lived in this beautiful house donated to us by an old lady who supported artists. We did little three-character plays. I directed some. I sold ads for some. I knew that something was being born."[17] The entire Streep clan dutifully traveled to see each performance, and Henry and Mary maintained the steadfast support they had always given their children in whatever they wanted to do—which was fortunate for Meryl, who was paid only $48.00 a week!

Despite her enthusiasm, rural theater was often a frustrating experience. Audiences were small and of mixed opinions about such esoteric drama. "You could hear the snoring in the bar and snowmobiles outside," she vividly remembers.[18]

Six months in the backwoods was enough to convince Meryl that if she wanted to pursue an acting career, she would need professional training to excel. "I knew that it was not enough to be an actress in the snows of Vermont. If I was going to do this thing, I ought to do it right. I decided to go to grad school."[19]

3
The Making of a Legend

If one is serious about a stage career, there are only two schools to consider: Juilliard and Yale. Meryl applied to them both. The fiercely independent spirit and contempt for snobbish elitism that had manifested itself at Vassar now determined her choice.

"Juilliard had this very uppity, expensive application that finally added up to $50.00. Yale's application was $15.00 and I was making $48.00 a week. So I wrote Juilliard a snotty letter saying 'this just shows what kind of cross-section of the population you get at *your* school.'"[1]

Meryl then applied to Yale and was given a three-year scholarship. The scholarship, while somewhat generous, just barely met expenses; to supplement it, she took jobs as a waitress and typist.

Robert Brustein, the innovative dean of the School of Drama and director of the Yale Repertory Theater, had developed an impressive reputation and a venturesome repertory company. Aspiring actors struggled to enroll, both to work under Brustein and for the opportunity to appear before the New York drama critics that regularly attended the performances looking for fresh faces and promising talent.

Meryl was determined to succeed. For her, Yale represented a point of no return. She immediately auditioned for Brustein. For her reading, she chose the scene from *Streetcar* that she had read for Atkinson; perhaps lightning would strike twice. And it did. Intrigued, Brustein asked her to read selections from *The Merchant of Venice*.

Despite a determination to persevere once she had made a decision, Meryl was still very shy and reluctant to compete aggressively with the other students for leading roles. Director Tom Haas placed her on academic probation during her first semester. "He said I was holding back my talent out of fear of competing with my fellow students," explains Meryl. "There was some truth in that, but there was no reason to put me on warning. I was just trying to be a nice guy, get my MA and get out of drama school."[2]

The message of Haas' warning was crystal clear: if she wanted to remain at Yale, she would have to assert the very competitiveness that she had so readily shucked at Vassar.

But Meryl thrived in that environment, winning leads in many of the school's productions. In her three years at Yale, she played an average of twelve to fifteen roles a year. Her repertoire, which ranged from ingenues to octogenarians, challenged and broadened her dramatic talent. Before long, she came to the attention of the faculty as something rare, even among a select group of highly talented actors and actresses. As Robert Lewis, drama professor, recalls, "Whenever she did a scene, you wished that the author were there to see it."[3]

Meryl's roles soon included several in the Repertory Theater: Bertha in Strindberg's *The Father*, Helena in *A Midsummer Night's Dream* and a wizened cripple in *The Idiots Karamazov*.

It was in *Idiots* that Meryl first displayed her talent for comedy, and this led to a number of comedic roles while at Yale; it also revealed her feisty, irrepressible nature. She had become so adept in winning roles and stealing scenes from her fellow students, that Haas now had to caution her to tone down her performances to avoid eclipsing the other actors in the play. Meryl did so, suppressing her resentment. Even in her restrained performance, she completely dominated the play, whirling madly in a wheelchair on the tiny stage. At the curtain call, she exacted her revenge on Haas. When the audience continued to applaud, Meryl wheeled herself back and forth on stage, shouting, "Go home! Go home!" then feigned a heart attack. The audience loved it and roared its approval.[4]

Albert Innaurato and Christopher Durang, the authors of the play and Meryl's classmates, were enthralled with her performance. "She invented the part," says Innaurato, "marvelously transforming herself into that eighty-year-old character. She even sang a Barbra Streisand parody — and she pulled it off. She's a genius."[5] Mel Gussow, theater critic of the *New York Times*, was another delighted spectator of her portrayal of "a babbling, decrepit old crone. It was a daring performance." As a result of his unqualified praise, other critics began to attend her performances and echoed his opinion. Unfortunately, Meryl never again had a role in school that revealed to full advantage her astonishing range and versatility.

As she showed a propensity toward madcap burlesque as well as drama, she came into increasing demand for major roles in the Yale Repertory Theater. Christopher Durang, a fellow student who went on to become a brilliant satiric playwright, remembers that "Meryl was Yale's leading lady. The School recognized her remarkable talent and worked her unmercifully."[6]

The endless casting led to exhaustion and an incipient ulcer. She lost weight under the strain of the constant pressure of various roles, and keeping up with her studies as well as two part-time jobs. "It was terribly intense," Meryl recalls. "Those years made me tired, crazy, nervous. I was constantly throwing up from the pressure. Sometimes I felt like saying, 'I can't do it anymore,' but the teachers would just say, 'You think this is bad, wait until you get out of here, will you have problems!'"[7]

Perhaps the most exasperating aspect of Yale to Meryl was the constant turnover of the faculty, each with his own pet acting technique. "Every year there'd be a *coup d'etat*. The new guy would come in with the new people and say, 'Whatever you learned last year, don't worry about it. This is going to be a completely new approach.'"[8] To Meryl, this constant barrage of new "gurus," each preaching the "one true way" was insufferable.

It was a schizophrenic period where she fluctuated between feelings of creative elation and a nagging sense of the absurdity of drama as a profession. Not the least of her frustrations was the conflicting, often absurd, methods taught by these transient drama professors. Her first year, the emphasis was on "improvisational techniques," in which the class did a version of Chekhov's *The Three Sisters*. She remembers most clearly of that experience the use of numbers as dialogue: One of her lines was "Three, five, five, five, seven, two, eight." Her second year, the rage was "emotional recall" by a teacher who "delved into personal lives in a way that I found obnoxious."[9]

From this mishmash of instruction, Meryl wisely selected the techniques that would prove most useful in her subsequent career: how to diagram a play, how to analyze a character, and most important, developing a confidence in her ability to interpret a character that was best suited to her talent. Once, when a director wanted to stage Bertolt Brecht's *Edward the Second* as a circus conceit, he wanted Meryl to wear a trapeze outfit with beads on her breasts and crotch. Meryl was adamant that the role of the queen did not warrant what was tantamount to a sexist approach; Meryl wore the costume, but without the beads.[10]

Despite the exhausting schedule and the egotism of members of the faculty, Meryl enjoyed the challenging roles and the free expression of pure creativity fostered at Yale. A fellow student, Joe Grifasi, remembers how impressed he was with Meryl's mastery of impromptu performances. There was one production by the Repertory Theater where an actor missed his cue, leaving Meryl in the worst predicament that can befall an actor — alone on the stage with no lines. Rather than stand there with egg on her face, she improvised. "The setting was a psychiatrist's office and Meryl walked around, picking up objects and finally peering intently at the Rorschach inkblot pictures on the wall. Then she looked at the audience as if she had discovered a major flaw in her character and burst into tears."[11]

Out of that three-year ordeal emerged a Yale legend: over forty roles, many of them memorable ones in the Yale Repertory Theater, and virtually unanimous praise from the faculty and her peers. Robert Lewis still remembers seeing Meryl as Alma in Tennessee Williams' *Summer and*

Smoke: "It was certainly the best I ever saw that part played, and that's a reaction you don't usually feel when students do scenes. It was like looking into somebody else's life."[12] One of her fellow students, now a successful actor in his own right, still recalls his amazement at her range in *Idiots Karamozov*. "It was really the most imaginative farcical performance I've ever seen."[13]

Brustein was so impressed with Meryl that he asked her to stay with the Repertory Theater after graduation. But Meryl had other priorities. For one thing, despite the scholarship and her part-time jobs, she still owed Yale $4000; for another, she wanted to go to New York and test her skills in the "real" theater world. She had grown weary of the academic pressure cooker, the teachers' endless imposition of a variety of techniques on her style, and even the praise and success.[14]

She had had enough of academics judging her with their pads and pencils on their laps. She longed for the two-way communication with a live audience, the interaction between actor and audience. This favored child of over a dozen college directors, now armed with a Master's in Fine Arts from one of the most prestigious drama schools in the country, was ready for the big time. There was only one place to find what she was seeking.

New York.

4
The Crucible

Most of the thousands of young actors and actresses that journey to New York with high hopes spend frustrating months sending their pictures around to agents and attending endless auditions. Most find their high expectations foundering in the bitter, cutthroat competition. They either go on unemployment or find menial jobs as dishwashers, waitresses or messengers, trying to stretch out their meager funds until the "break" comes. A fortunate few will find an occasional modeling job, television commercial or even a short-run, off-off–Broadway play where they remain anonymous to the critics, seen by only the few patrons that frequent those small theaters. By and large, they eventually lose heart and return to the obscurity whence they came.

In this grim, dismal world, Meryl longed to test her professional skills. Each step thus far had been an unqualified success: the Star of Vassar, the darling of countless directors, the Legend of Yale; each had been a slightly more demanding challenge with somewhat more critical audiences, but she had dazzled each in turn. But Meryl looked to New York as the only legitimate testing ground for her talent.

After the pressure and grind of Yale, it was a challenge that she savored, despite the dire warnings of the Yale faculty. "I found it to be great, everything they said it wouldn't be. It was very liberating when I got out to find that you're not competing with twenty-four people but with 20,000 others."[1] She was twenty-six and held an MFA from Yale. With these credentials, she set what would have been an unrealistic deadline to someone else: "I thought, 'I'm staring my new career. I better make it next year.'"[2]

Although she did not find the dreadful situation that her professors predicted, jobs were scarce enough that mass auditions were conducted by the Theater Communications Group, which provided a service to theaters, especially regional theaters outside of New York, to supply professional actors looking for parts. It was an obligatory stop for all drama school graduates, or those actors tired of beating their heads against doors that would not open. Meryl recollected recently that "we had a class at Yale on how to audition for TCG. It was unbelievable. Everybody had two

18

pieces—the serious one, and the comic one. The Shakespeare and the modern."[3]

Meryl stayed overnight in New York the day before the TCG audition. Now the applause from New Haven sounded distant indeed as she faced the first challenge of her professional career. She had occasionally auditioned in New York while still at Yale and loathed the cattle-call atmosphere. Perhaps these doubts accounted for what she did the next morning: "I woke up, looked at the clock and went back to sleep. I didn't go."[4]

Perhaps she was weary of having to exude unstinting optimism, or it may have been the nagging doubts that had followed her throughout her three years at Yale: Could her extraordinary success have been too easy? Was she nothing more than a promising amateur? Would the unbroken string of successes founder in the harsh reality of professional theater?

Meryl may have been the victim of self-doubt, but her decision was based on more than just an attack of nerves; acceptance within the TCG would mean leaving New York to the obscurity of regional theater, not unlike her experiences in summer stock in Vermont. If she was going to make it in the theater, she was determined to make it *in* New York.

Fearing she had ruined her chances, that afternoon she rushed to Rosemarie Tickler of the prestigious Public Theater. Nervously, Meryl begged her for an audition. When Tickler asked her why she had not gone to the TCG audition, Meryl described her ulcer trouble, realizing how lame her excuse sounded. Tickler looked at her for a long moment; she had seen thousands of anxious newcomers whose fears had cost them promising careers in the theater. Finally, she said, "All right. I may have something for you."

Rosemarie Tickler's "something" was nothing less than an audition for Joseph Papp's production of *Trelawny of the Wells*. Papp, famous as the impresario who brought Shakespeare to Central Park through the creation of the New York Shakespeare Festival, was one of the theater's most innovative and exciting directors. Novice and veteran actors clamored to be included in his productions. After hearing Meryl read, Papp offered her the role of Miss Imogen Parrot in *Trelawny*. That morning, Meryl feared she had thrown away her theatrical career; that evening, she had her first stage role in one of the most prestigious repertory companies in New York. It had to be one of the most auspicious beginnings to anyone's stage career.

Trelawny, with which Papp chose to open the 1975–76 season, was poorly received by the critics. They play had been written in 1898 for the London stage and did not adapt itself to the modern American theater. It was an affectionate sketch of backstage life among a group of thespians in a failing troupe. Although the critics panned the "creaking old play," Meryl received favorable mention as Miss Imogen Parrot, one of the troupe's more successful and eccentric alumnae. Stanley Kauffmann of *The New*

Republic found that "the most agreeable members of the 'Wells' company are John Lithgow, Meryl Streep and Marybeth Hurt." *Newsweek*'s Jack Kroll acknowledged the cast as "a warm and immensely winning ensemble." Meryl benefitted not only from the opportunity to appear in the Vivian Beaumont Theater in Lincoln Center, but also from a new friendship with Lithgow and Hurt.

Another result of the small part in *Trelawny* was her association with Papp. He was so impressed with her handling of the role that he immediately cast her in a twin bill when *Trelawny* closed in November. The two plays presented a unique challenge for Meryl: in Tennessee Williams' *27 Wagons Full of Cotton*, she was to play a 200-pound Southern slattern, while in *A Memory of Two Mondays*, by Arthur Miller, she portrayed a svelte New York secretary. Prior to the audition for *27 Wagons*, Meryl had rushed into the ladies' room to stuff tissue paper into her dress and affected what she herself termed "an outrageously overdone Southern accent" as she read for director Arvin Brown. The device worked and she was immediately hired.

So adroitly did she handle the two roles — one in the afternoon and the other in the evening — that few in the audience knew that the same actress was playing both the slovenly bovine and the sexy ingenue. As Meryl recalls, "It was a great showcase for an actress. In one play I was very fat; I did all kinds of padding and prosthetic breasts. In the other, I was a completely different person. What the people saw fed into what I wanted for myself — which was not to be typed."[5]

A Memory of Two Mondays revolves around the frustrations of clerical workers trapped into dull and mechanical jobs. It is a touching and often funny play in which the workers are portrayed with compassion rather than debasement. Meryl played Patricia, a secretary who is one of the fourteen office workers. With such a large cast, she received little individual attention from the critics, although Brendan Gill of *The New Yorker* found her "uncannily slender and brunette after her blowsy-blonde roundness in *27 Wagons*."

But in Tennessee Williams' *27 Wagons Full of Cotton*, she was one of only three characters, and received unanimous praise for her depiction of Flora, the slow-witted, passionate wife of an elderly cotton gin owner. The play (which was adapted for the movie *Baby Doll*) is a delightful Southern tall tale in which greed, cunning and stupidity are sharply etched. The elderly cotton gin owner has burned down the gin of a neighboring syndicate of cotton farmers to secure more work for his own gin, then offers his plump wife as a bribe to the suspicious syndicate manager. Brendan Gill called her "sensationally effective." Clive Barnes of the *New York Times* was even more enraptured with Meryl: "In both plays, Meryl Streep is a knockout — sexy in a womanly rather than girlish fashion, and terribly funny." Walter Kerr, also of the *New York Times*, enjoyed watching Meryl "studiously slap away most believable mosquitoes, splay her legs like a rag doll, twist an evasive but sinuous toe to keep the porch swing rocking rhythmically, count her thoughts on her fingers, clutch her oversize white purse as she weighs inadvertent betrayal against what is happening to her face." Harold Clurman of *The Nation* joined the chorus, saying she "projects complexity with dumbness; low-grade sensuality, animal simplicity striving for articulate thought, a sneaky vindictiveness as a form of unconscious rebellion."

The twin bill at the Phoenix Theater was a spectacular success. Reflecting on her first big break, Meryl has said, "This sort of thing is done all the time, but to do it in the same night was considered impressive."[6]

Impressive, indeed. In addition to the critics who regularly praised her performances, Joseph Papp was the most ecstatic. He recognized her gift for constant creativity, calling Meryl the most remarkable actress that he'd had at the Public Theater. "There are only a few people around I would call pure actors. Meryl is one. That means that the entire body is an instrument that is used constantly to serve a particular character . . . And she takes tremendous risks. . . . There are certain actors who would never play a negative role because they fear that the audience would not like them. But Meryl doesn't care, and she violates her classic beauty constantly."[7]

As at Vassar and Yale, Meryl's incredible success continued as she became the star of that season, appearing in an unprecedented seven plays her first season, with a leading role in six. She and Marybeth Hurt received laudatory comments in the spring of 1976 for clearly conceived interpretations of prototypical Southern belles in the Phoenix Theater's revival of William Gillette's *Secret Service*, in which she appeared with her other good friend from *Trelawny*, John Lithgow.

Suddenly, everyone in the theater was talking about this bright new talent with the Faye Dunaway face, mispronouncing her last name as "Strep"; reporters began calling for interviews, describing her as the "classical face that at times appears to be all cheekbones."[8]

At the end of the season, her first year on the professional stage was crowned with receiving the Outer Critics Circle Award, the Drama Desk Award, a nomination for a Tony for her performance in *27 Wagons* (she lost out to Shirley Knight for *Kennedy's Children*), and a Theatre World Award for both *27 Wagons Full of Cotton* and *A Memory of Two Mondays*.

Meryl's first year in professional theater had been a phenomenal success. Gone were any remaining fears about years of struggle in anonymity; instead, she was the hottest new star of the season. Her career had been an unbroken line of praise from increasingly authoritative theater people astonished at her seemingly unbounded talent. A parade of successes had followed her from Vassar to Yale to New York.

Meryl was modest about what many in the theater considered an unprecedented year for a rookie actress. "I've been shot with luck since I came to this city," she conceded to a *New York Times* reporter. "It's that thing where people say 'You're in the right place at the right time,' and I was."[9]

If Meryl was modest, others were not inclined to dismiss her talent so easily. Joseph Papp was so impressed with her that he invited her to join the New York Shakespeare Festival that summer; Papp's productions in Central Park's Delacorte Theater were widely regarded as some of the most exciting theater in New York.

To Meryl, Papp's invitation was as important a tribute to her talents as the awards she had received that spring, and she immediately accepted. It was a decision that would profoundly affect not only her professional career, but her up-to-now moribund personal life as well.

5
Love—and Tragedy

Under Joseph Papp's exacting guidance, Meryl performed even more brilliantly than she had at the Phoenix Theater. She immediately attracted critical praise for her "subtle, coquettish, altogether delightful"[1] French Princess Katherine in *Henry V* and the "impressive, moralistic"[2] Isabella in *Measure for Measure*, considered by many critics to be among the finest performance of the season.

While playing in *Measure*, she co-starred with John Cazale as the malevolent Angelo. Cazale, a Shakespearean actor best known for his film roles as the weak brother, Fredo, in *The Godfather* and the oddball bank robber in *Dog Day Afternoon*, was a dedicated, intense stage presence with the reputation among his peers as an "actor's actor" who lent quiet dignity to his roles. As the rehearsals continued, this sense of intensity drew him and Meryl closer together.

After the opening performance, the two went to a cast party, then breakfasted at the Empire Diner, an Upper West Side restaurant. Meryl had every reason to celebrate; the review by *New York Times* theater critic Mel Gusso raved about the play, singling out Meryl's "glowingly apparent versatility" and her ability to deliver a line in a way that "cuts like an icicle."

Meryl and John became lovers, moving into a loft in lower Manhattan. Her happiness was apparent to her friends. To those that knew both Meryl and John, their mutual attraction came as no surprise. Joe Grifasi, an old friend from Yale and the Phoenix, reflecting on why Meryl was so captivated by the forty-year-old John, has said, "It was a magnificent affair. Meryl admired his ability to cut through the crap and focus on the essentials. He was very careful to maintain his equilibrium."[3]

In addition to finally getting her personal life in order—or perhaps because of it—Meryl's career continued to skyrocket. She was deluged by reporters asking for interviews and found herself the most talked-about actress in New York that fall. Meryl was genuinely surprised that the critics should be so amazed at her phenomenal success; after all, her seven leads in one season was no more than she had done in a single year at Yale. "I've worked steadily here," she said in an interview. "I guess the odd thing would have been if I hadn't worked steadily."[4]

But her role as the chaste nun, Isabella, in *Measure* did present problems for the twenty-seven-year-old actress. One was convincing a cynical 1976 audience that purity of the soul was all that mattered to Isabella. Another was the physical problems presented by performing in Central Park. One night, thirty-one planes flew overhead during the first act alone. She was forced to scream out her lines to be heard.

The praise of New York critics eventually brought her to the attention of Hollywood producers. Richard Roth was anxious to have her portray the title role in 20th Century–Fox's *Julia*, based on Lillian Hellman's book *Pentimento*. While Meryl was still performing in *Measure*, Director Fred Zinnemann called to invite her to London, where filming was scheduled to start in September 1976. Yet another page had been added to the Streep legend: with just one year of experience on the stage, she was offered a co-starring role with Hollywood's top screen actress, Jane Fonda. It was an opening that many stage actresses must wait years for, and Meryl jumped at it.

Upon arriving in London for three weeks of shooting, Meryl found a very different situation. Although Zinnemann was unconcerned about the age span necessary for the character of Julia for the film, the producers felt that opposite Fonda, Meryl would look too young on screen. Instead, they offered her the role of Anne-Marie Travers, a self-centered socialite friend of Hellman. Meryl accepted the disappointment philosophically. The truth was that she was eager to accept *any* part in the film. She had decided that if she was going to break into films, she wanted to do so in an important one, and *Julia* certainly qualified. *Julia* also allowed her to make a personal statement about her political and social beliefs; the film shed a strong and positive light over women for a change. "The heart of the movie is the friendship between two women," she told reporters in London. In analyzing her own character's part, Meryl added, "Anne-Marie is very jealous of Julia and Lillian's friendship and hints that they are lesbians. She's an obnoxious character who wants to cash in on Lillian's playwriting success."[5] It was a role Meryl played to the hilt.

Her first day on the set, Meryl felt pangs of doubt. Would she ruin her first—and perhaps last—break into films? Another cause for anxiety was the wrench of her first separation from John, whose own career commitments had prevented him from accompanying her to England.

She quickly found that shooting a movie was an altogether different experience from the familiar world of the stage, and her nervousness was apparent. "The part in the movie came out of the blue. I thought I had perpetrated some sort of great hoax, that they would find out I was a charlatan."[6]

Sensing her anxiety, Fonda took Meryl under her wing from the first moment she arrived on the set, guiding her through the tortuous filming process. "Jane was very generous and understanding to a neophyte like me," she would later recall. "I was totally disassembled on the first day of shooting, which happened to be my biggest scene with Jane. But Jane took care of me and kept telling them they weren't lighting me enough."[7]

To Meryl, Jane Fonda was the archetypal modern woman balancing her private life with a career and social and political commitments. "I like her perspective," she once told a reporter. "She seems happy, together, committed to what she believes in."[8] By film's end, she and Fonda had become fast friends.

Although Meryl was only on screen in two short scenes, *Julia* was an excellent vehicle in which to make her film debut. It is Lillian Hellman's moving remembrance of an American woman of extraordinary heroism involved in the anti–Nazi underground of prewar Germany and Austria. Fred Zinnemann remained unusually true to the book, which has a strong emotional effect. Meryl was particularly pleased with the scene of the final meeting between Julia and Lillian. "It's unique because here are just two women talking, which you never see on the screen. Outside of Bergman's films, you never see women *really* talking to each other. It's never been thought important enough."[9]

As impressed as Meryl was with the film, the cast and crew had ample opportunity to be impressed with Meryl as well. Once, during a break in filming, she accompanied John Glover, who plays her brother in the film, to a party at a friend's house. Glover remembers that Meryl "had a sort of magnetism coming out of her. We played a game called Adverbs, where you have to do things in the manner of the word. She acted out someone getting up in the morning, going to the window and how she felt. Meryl did it so perfectly that everyone shouted out the word 'beautiful' at the same time."[10]

Returning to New York, Meryl was in more demand than ever, and was immediately cast as the precocious maid Dunyasha in Rumanian director Andrea Serban's unorthodox staging of Chekhov's *The Cherry Orchard*, which opened February 17, 1977, at the Vivian Beaumont Theater.

Serban had assembled a highly talented cast to provide the exuberance that he sought for the production, including Raul Julia as the former serf Lopakhin, Irene Worth as Madame Ranevskaya and Meryl's longtime friend Marybeth Hurt as Anya. Serban conceived of the play as a very physical one; Irene Worth was distraught on the floor in one scene, and Meryl's own part called for nothing less than calisthentics. Meryl found Serban's intense style of directing and urging of his cast to take risks with their characters to be a refreshing challenge. Not the least of Meryl's excitement was an opportunity to work with her brother, Harry, who had established his own dance company and choreographed the waltz sequences in the play.

The critics were torn between enthusiasm for the superb cast and dismay at Serban's unorthodox staging, which resulted in a stark, almost empty stage and looming backgrounds full of heavy-handed symbolism. Although her role as the amorous maid was a fairly small one, Meryl's performance carried the bulk of the comedy as her character pursued a hapless valet, intent on seducing him. *Newsweek*'s Jack Kroll observed that "the brilliant Meryl Streep as the maid Dunyasha apes the manners of her superiors with extravagant flutterings and faintings; thus, her little behavioral revolution sardonically prefigures other revolutions."

Unfortunately, the critics' irritation with what they considered Serban's misunderstanding of Chekhov's concept of comedy colored their perception of Meryl's role. While Walter Kerr and Clive Barnes of the *New York Times* extolled the boldness of the play, others proved more caustic. Stanley Kauffmann, in the *New Republic*, complained of the farcical horseplay. "Shyness in the maid Dunyasha is cartooned into constant drawer-dropping." Similarly, Brendan Gill of the *New Yorker* found that "to our dismay, we see Dunyasha somersaulting voluptuously over the valet she is in pursuit of, doing a partial striptease, tripping over her discarded undergarments, and finally tackling the valet and hurling him full length on the ground as if they were on a football field. That, shall we say, is not Chekhov."

Despite the mixed reviews, Meryl enjoyed the opportunity to give full range to her comedic talent. She also savored the exhilaration of being in a daringly different interpretation of the classic play.

The Cherry Orchard was in the final days of its sold-out run when the Chelsea Theater Center invited Meryl to replace Shirley Knight as the leading lady in the revival of Bertolt Brecht's musical comedy *Happy End*. With a chance to star in her first Broadway production, Meryl waited impatiently until Servan found her replacement, then immediately entered rehearsals. When Knight abruptly left the play on April 3, director Michael Feingold closed the production, scheduling its reopening at the Marvin Beck Theater on April 12. Although she only had a week to prepare for the part, Meryl had played the role of the female lead, Lt. Lillian Holiday ("Hallelujah Lil"), while at Yale; by the time the play reopened, she was eager to begin the part.

Happy End had originally been written in 1929 to capitalize on the success of *The Three-Penny Opera*, and centered around the attempt of a Salvation Army lass to reform a group of Chicago thugs in 1915. "Lil" is drummed out of the Salvation Army for falling in love with Bill Cracker, the leader of the gang, but she converts them all and is reinstated.

The production was plagued with problems from the beginning. In addition to Knight abruptly leaving the play, Christopher Lloyd, as Bill Cracker, tore several tendons in his knee during dress rehearsal, having to be replaced by Bob Gunton at the last moment. A week later, Gunton contracted the measles, necessitating a premature ·return by Lloyd, who hobbled around the stage on crutches. Despite these traumas, Meryl relished the chance to sing and dance for the first time since leaving Yale. She also enjoyed the opportunity to work with old friends; Yale classmate Joe Grifasi had a good comic part as a Salvation Army officer prone to fainting spells.

By the time that Meryl left the play in July, she had established herself with the audience, cast and critics alike. The *New Yorker* stated that "Meryl Streep, beautiful and charming, gives a star performance as Hallelujah Lil. Her song 'Surabaya Johnny' was well sung and very well acted, deservedly bringing down the house." Clive Barnes of the *New York Times* added, "The performance of the show comes from Meryl Streep as Hallelujah Lil. She is a knock-out. She sings and acts with utmost sweetness, and enormous style. She alone would make *Happy End* worth seeing."

But the mixed reviews that were to plague her career appeared in *Saturday Review*; touching upon the painstaking thoroughness of her preparation and technique, the review alluded to her "arrogant coldness" and the fact that "she seems not so much rehearsed as programmed."

A film commitment forced Meryl to leave the show at the end of July. The film was a CBS special, *The Deadliest Season*, a searing indictment of violence in professional hockey. Meryl played the deeply troubled wife of a professional hockey player (Michael Moriarty) accused of manslaughter during a fight on the ice. When it aired that summer, it swept the prime-time viewing charts.

Meryl was attracting increasingly favorable critical and public attention. Within two short years, she had been touted as the most talented newcomer to the New York stage where she had starred in an extraordinary seven major productions; she had had a part in a highly successful film; and she had made her television debut in a movie where she was seen by more people in a single night than had attended all of her stage appearances combined. But her mercurial career was just beginning.

Because of the critical acclaim she had received for her roles in *Julia* and *The Deadliest Season*, Michael Cimino cast her as Linda in his production of *The Deer Hunter*, a controversial epic of the Vietnam War. Typically, she played down the significance of her second film in less than a year. "They needed a girl between the two guys and I was it,"[11] she told the reporters who increasingly called for interviews.

To her delight, John was cast as Stan. The role was another weak, unstable character, so out of sync with his true nature, but one that he had almost patented in his brief career.

The film is set in a small Pennsylvania mill town, and is the story of three friends who enlist in the Army and go to Vietnam. The central character is Michael (Robert De Niro). Michael is a loner who lives by a strict code of honor, exemplified by his insistence on firing only one shot when hunting a deer.

The three soldiers are captured by the Viet Cong and forced to play

Russian roulette by their captors. During the game, Michael lulls the Cong into carelessness by repeatedly pulling the trigger while holding the gun to his forehead, then turning the gun on them. Michael rescues his friends and leads them back to safety. But Nick (Christopher Walken) is traumatized by the experience and refuses to leave Vietnam; instead he becomes a zombie-like creature in the demimonde of Saigon, playing Russian roulette for money. Michael returns to the United States sobered by his wartime experiences; he avoids the welcome home party and begins an ambiguous affair with Linda, Nick's girlfriend. Steven (John Savage) is a recluse in a veterans' hospital because of the loss of both legs. Michael forces him to accept reality and takes him home.

Perhaps from guilt at sleeping with his friend's girl, or a deep-seated loyalty, Michael returns to Saigon just as it is falling to the Communists, to find Nick. He risks his life by playing Russian roulette against Nick in a vain attempt to convince him to return home. But Nick is too far into the clutches of drug addiction and psychological trauma to return to his former life; he mechanically shoots himself in the head. Back home, the friends gather for Nick's funeral, trying to derive some meaning out of the senselessness of his death and their own experiences.

Immediately upon reading the script, Meryl realized that she was going to have difficulty justifying her character. Linda is the passive and vulnerable hometown sweetheart of a steelworker-turned-soldier. Meryl agonized over how to portray so one-dimensional a character; she wanted to make her memorable and evoke audience sympathy for Linda. In thinking out the character, she drew upon her own troubled adolescence. "I thought of all the girls in my high school who *wait* for things to happen to them; the kind who waits for someone to ask them to the prom, who waits for a lover to come back from war. Linda waits for a man to take care of her, to make her life happen."[12]

Meryl had initial misgivings about being able to work with her co-star, Robert De Niro; she had heard about his reputation for being volatile on the set and highly critical of his leading ladies. But they took an instant liking to each other, perhaps sensing the other's intense dedication to acting. De Niro was enthusiastic about Meryl from the beginning. "Women who are beautiful often let their beauty inhibit them," he told a reporter. "They tend to have no character. When a woman is beautiful and has an extra edge, like Meryl—it's nice."[13]

In the midst of their happiness at being able to spend months together on location in Steubenville, Ohio, tragedy struck John and Meryl. John discovered that he had bone cancer. They decided to keep his illness a secret until after shooting had ended. His portrayal of Stan was all the more remarkable in that he barely had the strength to complete his scenes, fighting for the energy to say his lines as the ravages of the disease exhausted him.

Back in New York, Meryl found herself besieged with enticing and lucrative offers for other films and television. But John's illness put a pall over what would otherwise have been an unbelievable dream.

That fall, instead of being able to stay in New York with John, she was committed to begin location shooting of the television miniseries *Holocaust* in Austria.

6
Conundrum

Holocaust was an ambitious gamble for NBC. Envisioned as a nine-and-a-half-hour miniseries, it would portray the harrowing agony of European Jews under Nazism from 1935 to 1945. The story centers around two families: the Weisses, well-educated Berlin Jews, and the Dorfs, the family of an ambitious S.S. officer. Producer Herbert Brodkin was able to convince NBC executives that the audience reaction would not be negative to the somber theme, and it could rival the phenomenal success of ABC's *Roots* the previous season.

Meryl played Inga, a Catholic woman who voluntarily follows her Jewish husband to a concentration camp. It was an important role that would impress itself on the audience; Inga was the only sympathetic German role in the entire production.

Those two-and-a-half months in Austria were torture for Meryl. She felt terribly guilty at not being in New York with John, but she needed the money; she still owed Yale $4000, and the medical bills for John's treatment were enormous. "I was going crazy," she recalled in an interview. "John was sick, and I wanted to be with him. But they just kept extending the damn thing. It was like being in prison for two months."[1]

Holocaust was an unhappy production for the entire cast, which found the shooting at the actual site of the Mathausen concentration camp oppressive. James Woods, who played Meryl's screen husband, remembered the feeling: "On the days we were working at Mathausen—the gas chamber, in particular—there was a lot of squabbling on the set. We felt so awful in a place like that, and we tended to take it out on the people we were working with, when, in fact, we were feeling this rage against the Nazis."[2] Once, Michael Moriarty, who portrayed Eric Dorf, ran from the set sobbing, "How could they? How could they?" Even veteran British actor Cyril Sharp had to repeatedly reshoot his lines, saying, "I don't think I can go on."

It was only months later, when John's condition became known, that her fellow cast members fully appreciated the emotional strain that Meryl was undergoing. Looking back on those days on location, co-star Fritz Weaver recalls: "In *Holocaust* she played a woman whose lover was imprisoned in a concentration camp. Meryl must have been living it twice, in the story and in real life. But there was not one moment of self-pity. She had tremendous professional devotion."[3]

Finally, the long weeks in Austria came to an end and Meryl returned to New York and the gravely ill John. Shocked at his physical deterioration, Meryl put her rapidly evolving career on hold to devote herself completely to his care.

Although the cancer had progressed rapidly by this time and doctors gave John only a few months to live, Meryl refused to give up hope, convincing herself that he would recover. She quietly paid the mounting bills with a stubborn optimism. As John grew weaker, he was moved to Sloan-Kettering Memorial Hospital. Meryl did everything she could to keep up his spirits. She did comic readings of the sports page in mimicry of television and radio announcers, and she urged old friends to come by to see him. Her mentor, Joseph Papp, was particularly touched by her devotion. "She took care of him as if there were nobody else on earth. She was always at his side. It was such a statement of loyalty, of commitment. She gave him tremendous hope."[4]

But her obstinate refusal to accept the reality of John's condition availed her nothing; on March 13, 1978, John slipped into a coma and died.

Meryl grieved privately, trying to come to terms with her devastating personal loss. Sympathetic friends kept in touch, but she withdrew behind a protective shell. "I was emotionally blitzed," she remembers. "It was a selfish period of trying to incorporate what had happened in my life."[5]

Ironically, at this moment of despair, NBC aired *Holocaust* on four consecutive nights, making Meryl an overnight celebrity. She had been seen by an estimated 120 millions of people in her first major role, and the critics loved her. For NBC, the $6 million gamble had been a rousing success. The release was timed to coincide with Passover and the thirty-fifth anniversary of the Warsaw Ghetto Uprising. Critical controversy thus centered, not on the quality of the performances, but on the treatment of the subject. Critics disagreed over whether the "docudrama" accurately portrayed history or distorted it. Did the subject lend itself to dramatization, or was the Holocaust trivialized in the attempt? While critics ranged in their reviews from *Newsweek*'s "highly salutary video event" to *Time*'s "banal mockery of human suffering," they were unanimous in their praise of the cast, which included an unusually large number of professionally trained stage actors and actresses, such as Ian Holm of the Royal Shakespeare Company, Rosemary Harris from the Broadway stage and Meryl herself. Because critical attention focused on whether the portrayal of the Holocaust was accurate or exploitative, it did not generally comment on individual performances. But *New York* Magazine was particularly impressed by Meryl: "Special note has to be taken of the performance of Meryl Streep who is heroically loyal to her Jewish husband to the very end." The National Society of Film Critics later voted her Best Supporting Actress in a Television Dramatic Special.

Audience reaction echoed the praise of the critics. While it did not equal the ratings success of *Roots*, capturing only 49 percent of the viewer audience as opposed to *Roots'* 66 percent, some 120 million viewers were gripped by the emotionally wrenching miniseries. Most Jews responded favorably; Rabbi Abraham Weiss of New York's Yeshiva University led a group of students to NBC studios in a demonstration of support, and the Anti-Defamation League of B'nai B'rith singled out Meryl's performance by presenting her with a special award.

But critical acclaim and instant celebrity status were not enough to assuage Meryl's depression over John's death. Her brother, Harry, moved in with her to ease her loneliness. Shortly after John's funeral, a bizarre incident added further torment to Meryl's grief. A former girlfriend of John's arrived from California and showed them a lease agreement she and John had signed five years before. Although the woman and John had never lived together in the apartment, she claimed it and evicted Meryl and Harry. Within three weeks, Meryl had lost both John and their home.

Friends constantly urged her to return to work in the weeks that followed John's death. As Meryl sought to put the shattered pieces of her life back together, she sensed they were right. Her art had been her central focus before John; perhaps it would prove to be her salvation again.

She was offered the role of Leilah, a deeply troubled Mt. Holyoke graduate, in Wendy Wasserstein's *Uncommon Women and Others* on PBS's "Theater in America" series. The production aired on May 24, 1978, to favorable reviews. It was another strong woman's role of a type Meryl felt comfortable performing.

In this ironic, affectionate comedy, five college friends attend a reunion several years after graduation. As each describes her post-college activities, she reveals bewilderment and disappointment with her subsequent life. It is a period of ambivalence and uncertainty for all of them. At graduation, they had all looked forward to entering the larger world beyond the campus, expecting a world of expanded goals and options for women. Now, they have lost their grand expectations, settling instead for smaller dreams with no sign of a belief in, or commitment to, anything. Meryl's face was drawn and tense from the strain of John's final days and the suffering she had gone through in the intervening weeks, but Leilah is a tormented soul and Meryl's face was just right for the part.

Now Meryl felt ready to take on something more challenging. Alan Alda, star of television's hit series M*A*S*H, had written a screenplay about the corruption of an idealistic young senator. He would play the senator, but the female lead had yet to be signed. After tentative negotiations by her agent, Sam Cohn of ICM, the lead went to Barbara Harris as his wife, but Universal signed Meryl to play the senator's mistress.

In June, she traveled to Baltimore and Washington to begin shooting Alda's film *The Seduction of Joe Tynan*. As Tynan's mistress, Meryl plays Karen Traynor, a sly, educated, rich Southern civil rights lawyer. Once more Meryl had the challenge of making an essentially unsympathetic character comprehensible to the audience.

As Tynan, Alda portrays a charismatic, liberal senator who becomes seduced by presidential ambitions and a beautiful woman. The film centers upon the ethical and personal conflicts that beset Tynan: he has presidential aspirations that cause him to neglect his family; his ideals impel him to oppose the Supreme Court nomination of a Southern racist, although it will ruin the career of his political mentor; and his attraction to a civil rights lawyer threatens to destroy his marriage. Looking for an issue that will propel him into the national spotlight, he finds one in blocking the nomination of a blatant racist to the Supreme Court. Senator Birney (Melvyn Douglas) solicits Tynan's support in order to keep the nominee from running against Birney in the next election. Tynan agrees not to oppose the nomination, but must renege because of moral principles — and the urging of his staff, who see the issue as material to make Tynan a serious candidate for the Democratic party's nomination for president. As a result of Tynan's successful opposition, Birney's political career is ruined, and Tynan attracts favorable public and party attention.

During the confirmation hearings, Tynan works closely with an attractive, intelligent civil rights lawyer named Karen Traynor (Meryl). Their relationship rapidly develops into a passionate affair, which threatens his marriage, already shaky because of long absences from home. In addition, Tynan must confront the disaffection of his two children, who feel abandoned while he is in Washington for weeks at a time.

In the end, all of Tynan's problems are resolved; he is never really seduced by either power or Karen. He ends his affair with Karen, shores up his unstable marriage and makes peace with his children. The conflicts are all resolved in Tynan's favor; his ethical standards remain intact without his ever having to come to grips with the difficult issues involved. While the first half of the film focuses upon the hard choices involved in Tynan's pursuit of both public ambition and a private life, the film concludes with his achieving both without sacrificing either. He emerges at the Democratic National Convention as a leading candidate with the approval of his family.

Tynan was the best possible therapy for Meryl; she had no time to dwell upon her loss. After each day's shooting, she was so tired that she collapsed into bed. "I did it on automatic pilot," she recalls. "It seems as if I did it in another life."[6]

In Alda, Meryl found helpful support. Aware of the emotional strain she was undergoing, he was impressed with her professionalism and tried in every way possible to help her through the more difficult scenes. "She

As civil rights lawyer Karen Traynor, Streep faces down Alan Alda (as Senator Joe Tynan) in The Seduction of Joe Tynan.

looked at the movie as some kind of test," Alda remembers. "A test she had to pass. She was determined not to buckle."[7]

The most trying scenes were the passionate love scenes with Alda. Her old friend John Lithgow recalls one highly charged love scene she did with Alda. "It's a scene that demands tremendous high spirits and a great deal of sexual energy, and at that time, right after John Cazale had died, Meryl was in no mood for either. And she was embarrassed by the scene. She would perspire until she was dripping wet from embarrassment."[8]

Working on a good script in an important film was what Meryl needed to mend herself emotionally. She was grateful for the understanding of the cast and crew, especially Alda, but it did not completely salve her sense of loss. "I couldn't have worked with a more lovely, understanding person than Alan Alda," she once reflected, "but for some things there is no comfort."[9]

Critics were divided in their opinions on *Tynan*. On the one hand, they castigated the stale theme of political corruption, but on the other, they were intrigued by the subtle nuances that a superb cast brought to their characters.

Time's Frank Rich, while praising Alda for "taking the sanctimoniousness out of heroism," deplored the rehashing of trite views of the political milieu. "Not only do these dilemmas have the aura of the casebook about them," he wrote, "they are also resolved perfunctorily and predictably." Stanley Kauffmann called the film "an odd mixture of freshness and leftovers." Kauffmann found the theme of a man torn between family and ambition an all-too-familiar film standard, as in *Advise and Consent* and *The Best Man*, but he admired Alda's deft touch at revealing the daily routine of the Senate. "The senatorial atmosphere and the Washington byplay seem authentic, but what's really interesting is that the film deals with political *life*. It sensitively and effectively deals with the conflict between maintenance of ethics and the moulding of ambition in a realistic, but uncynical fashion."

The critics all had unreserved praise for the cast. Rip Torn made the most of a small role as an inebriate, libertine senator; Barbara Harris was dignified, yet warmly human as Tynan's long-suffering wife; and Melvyn Douglas expanded his part as a senile senator that Tynan must betray into a tour de force. But critical attention remained focused on Meryl. As Kauffmann commented: "Meryl's character development gives the film much of its credibility. Streep is at once a cunning politico, a blithe belle, and an uninhibited sex partner." Rich added: "Like Katherine Hepburn, she uses her regal beauty and bearing to make her sudden descents to earth all the more exciting." *New York*'s David Denby, while complimenting Melvyn Douglas, Barbara Harris and Alan Alda for excellent renderings of their characters, saved his highest praise for Meryl. "She is so fresh for us that each smile or dip of the head feels like a revelation. It is a pleasure to see her as a tough, wily, aggressive woman; indeed, the flashes of avidity breaking through her southern-lady's gaiety and charm in this role make one long for her to cast off niceness altogether." Even the caustic John Simon felt compelled to comment: "Meryl Streep manages the merry intelligence and cool seductiveness of Karen with perfect assurance." Many critics saw in Meryl's performance a style and grace that harkened back to an earlier Hollywood era. The *Washington Post*'s James Lardner noted that "from her first entrance in the film, she runs the show as few actresses have since the 1940s."

The scene that most captivated critics was when Alda and Meryl

exchange their first kiss. As she lowers her face to kiss Tynan in a long, slow
close-up, Denby commented, "Watching that sinuous swan neck, you hold
your breath — the moment is like some romantic epiphany from a thirties
classic." *Newsweek*'s Jack Kroll, in commenting on the same scene, added:
"Her eyes alone tell us more than most actresses could manage in an hour."

One critic summed up the feelings of all by saying, "The energy in this
movie comes from Meryl Streep as Karen Traynor. Streep is merely
superb; she ranges up and down the emotional scale with disarming ease
and becomes the center of attention whenever she is on screen."

Within weeks, Meryl began work on Woody Allen's new film, *Manhattan*. Whereas *Tynan* had been a satisfying role that provided Meryl the opportunity to develop the type of character she enjoyed playing, *Manhattan*
was not.

Manhattan is Woody Allen's moral narrative about his love affair with
New York. The film centers around the shallow lifestyles of New York's jet-
set of the 1970s. Their world is filled with status-seeking in the *belle monde*
of art and literature. In their studied posturing, they profess a love of art,
but they are incapable of loving other people as they drift in and out of
casual affairs in a desperate search for the "ideal love" to escape the banality of their lives. They spend their time narcissistically talking about their
neuroses and their unfinished novels and paintings, a mixed bag of "culture
junkies."

Issac Davis (Woody Allen) has just resigned in disgust from his job as
a television sitcom writer to return to writing his novel. Davis's ex-wife, Jill
(Meryl), who has left him for another woman, is writing a book on the
failure of their marriage that will expose him to public humiliation. To con-
sole himself, Issac is having a love affair with seventeen-year-old Tracy
(Mariel Hemingway). But Davis is enamoured with an abrasive, militantly
intellectual journalist, Mary Wilke (Diane Keaton), who is having an affair
with Issac's best friend, Yale (Michael Murphy). When Yale leaves Mary,
Issac breaks up with Tracy to begin a frustrating affair with Mary. Mary
eventually returns to Yale, and a contrite Issac rushes in panic to Tracy,
only to find her leaving for a year's study in London. She leaves Issac a
sadder-but-wiser man who must learn to look for life's meaning by becoming sensitive to other people's pain.

It was a frustrating role for Meryl, after the challenge of *Holocaust*, *The
Deer Hunter* and *Tynan*. She was dissatisfied that her small part did not
allow her to develop a sympathetic character, as she had in *Tynan*, and the
theme of narcissism offended her.

Manhattan inevitably led reviewers to compare it with the more
popular *Annie Hall*; it suffered by comparison. Stanley Kauffmann was
disappointed by the film's inability to evoke the commercialism-idealism
struggle presented at the outset. David Denby, while admiring Allen's
satire, found the characters' relationships too bland and poorly defined. In

his opinion, Allen did not develop the possibilities of romance and bit-
tersweet regret, nor the moods of anger, yearning and frustration present
in the film. Both, however, admired Allen's affecting moments when,
beneath the character's intellectual dialogue and obsession with art and
material comfort, their spiritual unease emerges.

Most critics hailed *Manhattan* as a brilliant revelation of Allen's newfound maturity as a film director, but a few were put off by his heavy-
handed moralizing, and rejected it as "serious comedy." John Simon considered the film "profoundly and multifariously dishonest" with "tongue-in-
cheek cynicism" and "a self-serving exaltation of Allen and his values . . .
self adulation and Manhattan boosting." David Denby, however, enjoyed
Allen's "powerful new movie" and his portrayal of New York as "a city of
infinite promise and frequent despair." He congratulated Allen for being
a consummate satirist of manners and intellectual fashion in "his harshest
. . . film yet." But Denby did find fault; he found Allen's moral tone to be
affected and unconvincing. ". . . I admire his 'new seriousness,' but I don't
much care for trite guidance-counselor commentaries."

The focus of critical attention was with Allen and his theme, but the
cast received favorable mention, especially the women. As Denby noted,
"Here the women characters have become fully rounded. Meryl Streep
doesn't have time to establish her character, but Mariel Hemingway, who
does, is a marvel. And Diane Keaton gives her boldest, most interesting
performances to date." Stanley Kauffmann was not inclined to be as
generous as Denby in assessing either the film or the acting of the cast.
"Somewhere in this mildly interesting, meandering script was an attempt
to write a serious comedy about a man trying to live by moral principles
in a world of gratification-as-ethics. But the film is so anxious to stay cool,
with every coolant that comes along, that the theme is lost."

Nor did the cast come off any better in Kauffmann's estimation. "Allen
is insufficient as actor and person to make either the performance or his
attractiveness convincing. The rest of the cast is mediocre to poor."
Michael Murphy was "like well-chosen wallpaper"; Mariel Hemingway was
"dull"; and Diane Keaton's familiar performance as a scatterbrained New
Yorker was merely "routine." Meryl was the only member of the cast to
receive even faint praise: "Meryl Streep does all that can be done with a
small, virtually unwritten part." Ironically, it was Diane Keaton that had
the opportunity to do what was Meryl's metier, to have the time to make
the shrill, tortured, self-conscious snob Mary into a sympathetic character.

While her role was severely limited and did not utilize her expressive
features and range, Meryl is at once chilling and funny in the scene when
she announces that she is leaving Allen, and then horrifies him by revealing
that she intends to write a book about their intimate life together. Although
she was on the set for only three days, Meryl served as an excellent
counterpoint to Keaton's agitated femininity.

But the nature of her role did not allow time for her to engender audience sympathy, a point that critics were quick to note. David Denby stated that she "stays around long enough to establish herself as a shrill woman of self-discovery." As Jill, she portrays a "castrating woman" and a "humorless valkyrie." Meryl had the misfortune to be trapped in between Keaton's zaniness and Hemingway's endearing honesty. All in all, Jill was a disappointing, virtually unnoticed role that did little for Meryl's career.

After completing her scenes for *Manhattan*, Meryl immediately entered rehearsals for *Taming of the Shrew* for Joseph Papp's New York Shakespeare Festival in Central Park. When asked by a *New York Times* reporter why she was returning to the festival, Meryl replied, "I like the continuity of being associated with one company."[10] But perhaps it was another step in her recovery, returning to the group that had brought her and John together.

Meryl was particularly pleased with the interpretation that Papp and director Wilford Leach gave to the play. She, Papp and co-star Raul Julia were dissatisfied with traditional renditions that portrayed Katherine being reduced to subservience to her future husband, Petruchio. Leach seemed embarrassed by the theme of wife-taming and of treating women as the husband's chattel. Changing the traditional conception of the play, when Kate makes her vow of submission to Petruchio at the wedding, Meryl placed her hand under Raul Julia's foot, but he then knelt, gently took her hand and kissed it.

Critics, however, were in no mood for Leach's innovations. As with *The Cherry Orchard*, they resented tampering with a classic. Perhaps John Simon's review in *New York* magazine best typified the critical response. Simon felt the play had the result of "making Kate into a kind of Jane Withers or *Our Gang* brat on the one hand, while, on the other, letting her be a subtle ironist and so reducing her to a flagrant self-contradiction . . . often allowing both Kate and Petruchio to carry on as if they meant none of this. Meryl Streep is an extremely interesting, often compelling actress, but her Kate—partly from bad direction, partly from ideological scruples—ends up as a thing of shreds and patches; some fine moments, but no cohesive interpretation. And one should not hear her mutter 'Oh, s--t.'" But Meryl was pleased with the play and that was what mattered most to her at the time.

As Meryl began to heal emotionally, her confidence also began to reassert itself; although she had been a professional actress for only two years, she had already formulated some definite ideas on the positive and negative aspects of her profession. On September 17, 1978, she received an Emmy for Outstanding Actress in a Limited Series for her role in *Holocaust*. Despite her appreciation of the honor, Meryl refused to accept it in person. "I don't believe performances should be taken out of context and put up against each other for awards," she told the press.[11]

Another of her strong beliefs centered around the perceptions of the public regarding a performance. Along with the critics, she had worried that the hoopla surrounding the broadcasting of *Holocaust* would overshadow the horror of the events depicted. As if to confirm her fears, on the day after the Emmy Awards ceremony, she was walking down the street. Several young men in a passing Volkswagen shouted, "Hey, Holocaust! Hey, Holocaust!" Despite the good intentions of those fans, Meryl was appalled. "Can you imagine reducing something that traumatic to shouting at an actress?" she told a reporter walking with her.[12]

Meryl had returned to work in good films and was again appearing on stage. She had received both critical success and the respect of her colleagues; indeed, she felt confident enough in her profession to publicly criticize its excesses. But her external assertiveness masked an internal vulnerability over the loss of John Cazale. Declining to answer journalists' questions concerning her private life with John, she would speak feelingly about his acting talent, saying, "I think he was an unsung actor."[13]

7
Resurrection

If the Emmy stabilized Meryl's career, an even more important event brought peace to her personal life.

She and Harry were vacating the apartment she had shared with John; Donald Gummer, a long-time friend of Harry's, offered to help them. A thirty-two-year-old, highly respected sculptor of huge wall pieces, architectural frameworks, and wooden geometric designs, Don had graduated from the Yale School of Design. He was also recently divorced. Meryl had been introduced to Don by Harry in the spring of 1978. "He and my brother had been friends for years and I had met Don two or three times," she confided. "But I honestly didn't remember him." Don was leaving for a world exhibition of his sculpture, and offered Meryl and Harry his studio loft in SoHo as temporary living quarters while he was away.

Meryl's schedule was hectic that spring and summer. In May, she went to Baltimore and Washington to complete scenes for *Tynan*, and in July she worked on Woody Allen's *Manhattan*. Don wrote her often from various places on the exhibition tour, and she wrote back; a friendship developed through the letters.

When Don returned to New York, he built a room for Meryl in the loft and urged her to stay after Harry left. They began attending art museums and plays together, discovering compatible values, especially a shared interest in a quiet social life. Gradually, they fell in love. In September 1978, Don and Meryl were married in a quiet outdoor ceremony at her parents' retirement home in Mystic, Connecticut. The service was attended by immediate family members and a few close friends.

Meryl was sensitive to her friends' surprise at her marriage just six months after John's death. "I didn't want to get over John's death," she explains. "No matter what you do, the pain is always there in some recess of your mind, and it affects everything that happens afterwards. But just as a child does, I think you can dissimilate the pain and go on without making an obsession of it."[1]

Of her decision to marry Don, she also told an interviewer, "It just seemed right. A lot of men have asked me to marry them, but it had never really seemed right before. He's a very private person, and he never says anything he doesn't mean. He's warm, strong, gentle, funny, kind, understanding and very creative. I couldn't live with someone who wasn't creative."[2]

After the marriage, they returned to the loft in SoHo and settled into quiet domesticity. Meryl and Don avoided the big "show biz" parties, preferring to entertain small groups of friends, usually fellow artists and actors, at home. Marybeth Hurt and Joe Grifasi were frequent guests; on such occasions, Meryl and Joe would perform impromptu comic skits. Don was aware of the difficulties that he would face being married to an actress who was rapidly attracting critical and public attention; there would be the constant pressure from autograph seekers and reporters asking for interviews and photo sessions, and the jealousy of actors' spouses over torrid love scenes that have destroyed more than one Hollywood marriage. But Don viewed these pressures confidently. "There are many different kinds of love," he once told a reporter. "Our is founded on a very deep-rooted feeling of trust. We're best friends."[3]

Meryl enthusiastically supported Don's assessment of their marriage, insisting her decision to marry was not the result of an emotional rebound. "I fell in love with Don fast," she said, "but I've known him for a long time. I had a definite reading about Don and myself very soon — and I was right. We're similar in a lot of ways. Don's work is solitary and he isolates himself from things, but he likes movies and theater, as I do. He also has a great sense of humor — and a sense of himself and his work that's imperturbable. The marriage is the best thing that has happened to me."[4]

It was fortunate that their marriage was so solidly based on a foundation of trust and mutual understanding of artistic temperment. Within weeks of her marriage, Meryl began work on *Kramer vs. Kramer*, her third film that year.

Word spread quickly throughout Hollywood and New York that *Kramer vs. Kramer* would be the hottest picture of the year. Adapted from the novel by Avery Corman, the movie concerns a man whose wife abandons him and their six-year-old son, only to return eighteen months later, generating a vicious custody battle. Although the book only sold 12,000 copies, producer Stanley Jaffe convinced Columbia Pictures to purchase the film rights for $200,000. After the success of such films as *Julia*, *An Unmarried Woman*, and *Annie Hall*, in which women were having their say on screen, Jaffe felt the time was ripe for a film that focused on the perspective of the husband in the dissolution of a marriage.

Ted Kramer is an aggressive executive of a prestigious advertising firm. He returns one night to his apartment, excited about his promotion to vice-president, only to find his wife Joanna packing to leave him. She can no longer live in his shadow, forced to suppress her own career ambitions to the roles of wife and mother. Ted is dumbfounded; he has been so immersed in his work that he has been oblivious to Joanna's increasing dissatisfaction. Joanna is so desperate to escape that she leaves their six-year-old son, Billy, with Ted.

Ted is initially so wrapped up in his own confused anger that he ignores the traumatic effects of the separation on Billy. His attempts to care for Billy as a suddenly single parent are at first clumsy, rejected by a sullen and resentful Billy, who blames Ted for his mother's sudden departure. Gradually, a tender relationship develops between father and son, in which fatherhood takes precedence over career ambitions. As a result, Ted's career suffers; eventually he is fired.

At this point, Joanna returns after an eighteen-month absence to ask Ted for custody of Billy. They have quietly become divorced, and she is now a self-confident, successful advertising executive in her own right, ready to reassume the role of mother. Ted is in a panic; he wants to fight for custody of his son, but he is unemployed and faces the court's prejudice in favor of the mother in custody suits. He scurries around New York, frantically seeking a job; he eventually finds one at a substantially reduced salary, and hires an attorney.

In the ensuing court battle, Ted and Joanna slowly come to understand one another for the first time. Neither is a villain; they are just two decent people whose goals drove them in opposite directions. Both Ted and Joanna are appalled to re-examine their life together and realize how little they knew one another. As the lawyers attempt to discredit one or the other, Ted and Joanna are traumatized by the experience and bury their mutual animosity in a newfound understanding.

The court awards custody to Joanna. In order for Ted to appeal the decision, his lawyer will have to put Billy on the witness stand, which Ted refuses to do. As Ted and Billy are painfully saying goodbye to each other the next morning, Joanna calls, asking Ted to meet her in the lobby. There she tells him that she cannot take Billy away from his father, that she is renouncing custody. From the catharsis of the divorce and custody struggle, Ted and Joanna have come to realize that Billy's happiness is the most important thing in their lives.

Jaffe wanted Dustin Hoffman to portray the father, Ted Kramer. Hoffman was interested in the part, but was committed to finish *Agatha* in England; therefore, production was delayed from April to September 1978. During that time, director Robert Benton rewrote the script a total of fourteen times to get just the right approach to Ted's dilemma.

Once Hoffman returned to the United States, casting calls went out for the role of the wife, Joanna Kramer. Rumors circulated that Kate Jackson, Dustin's current love interest and one of television's "Charlie's Angels," was assured the role, but a last-minute schedule conflict forced her to decline. Sam Cohn, Meryl's agent at ICM, was a personal friend of both Avery Corman and Robert Benton; he suggested that they consider

Streep in the role of Joanna Kramer in Kramer vs. Kramer.

Meryl for a part. Benton, who had been favorably impressed by her role in *Holocaust*, agreed and called her in for a reading for the role of Phyllis, one of Ted's one-night-stands.

Meryl had other ideas. After a series of supporting roles which had received favorable critical reviews, Meryl was ready to take on a leading role.

Hoffman, Jaffe and Benton met her in their hotel headquarters. They talked perfunctorily about the minor role, then Meryl began to tell them how she saw Joanna Kramer. Encouraged by the questions that they asked her, Meryl quickly warmed to the topic. The part appealed to her as a chance to embellish an essentially stereotypical woman's role and the

challenge to make the character more understandable to the audience. She
told them that Joanna Kramer, as originally written in the novel, was too
"evil," and the couple's conflicts too narrowly described. The audience
should really understand why she leaves and sympathize with Joanna when
she tries to regain custody of the child. When she at last gives up the boy,
Meryl said, it should be for the *boy's* sake, not her own. Only in this manner
could they present a more realistic situation.

Meryl left without anything said about giving her the role of Joanna,
but the interview had gone exceptionally well; after the first few minutes,
nothing further had been said about the part of Phyllis, and they seemed
receptive to her interpretation of Joanna.

In fact, Hoffman, Jaffe and Benton were so impressed with Meryl that
they immediately began yet another script revision that more closely followed her interpretation of the character of Joanna. Benton later recalled,
"As soon as Dustin and I were back on the street, we realized she was the
girl for us." Hoffman, in particular, was dissatisfied with Avery Corman's
"woman-hating" element in the book and sought a more balanced approach
to Joanna's angst; Meryl's conception of the part and his own meshed well.
He and Benton offered the role to Meryl.

The part hers, Meryl began a period of intense research. She fre-
quented the Upper East Side of New York where the Kramers were supposed to live, read the magazines that Joanna read—those with stories of
women with successful careers and home lives—and talked with friends
(including her own mother) about the tensions involved in balancing the
two lifestyles. After several weeks of exhaustive research, she felt that she
was inside the world of Joanna Kramer.

But getting inside the *mind* of Joanna Kramer was another matter. It
was a dilemma that would plague Meryl through most of the filming of the
picture.

As shooting began, Meryl approached working with co-star Dustin
Hoffman with some trepidation. After all, he had a reputation as a
"difficult" actor, one whose intensity in researching a role had caused tension and frequent arguments on the sets of his previous films. But Meryl
had an intensity and devotion to her art to match his own; she quickly won
Hoffman's respect and admiration.

Generally, Meryl and Hoffman worked well together. One exception
was an argument over the restaurant scene in which Joanna returns to demand custody of Billy. Meryl wanted the news to come late in the conversation, while Hoffman thought it would be more effective in the beginning,
as originally written. When Meryl played it her way, Hoffman became so
upset that he threw a glass against the wall. Benton thought Dustin's reaction lent just the right tone to the scene, and decided to leave it in the final
cut of the film. "I hated her guts," Hoffman confessed later, "but I respected
her. She's ultimately not fighting for herself, but for the scene. She sticks

to her guns and doesn't let anyone mess with her when she thinks she's right."[5]

Apart from that one incident, the two stars developed not only a compatible professional working relationship, but a personal friendship as well. Not that there weren't tensions on the set; numerous arguments arose between Hoffman, Meryl and Benton over script interpretations.

But, on the whole, it was a relaxed set, relatively free from friction between cast members. A reporter visiting the set noticed the laid-back relationship between Hoffman, Meryl and six-year-old Justin Henry, who played Billy Kramer. During a break in filming, Justin was eating a packed lunch with his parents, Hoffman was lying under a tree and Meryl was coping with yet another interview on the set. Suddenly, Hoffman shouted over at Justin, "Who do you want to live with, her or me?" Justin immediately replied, "Her! She's nicer." Hoffman feigned a pout. "Oh, yeah?" he yelled. "Work with her five more weeks and see what you say." It broke up the set.

Greater tension was avoided between the co-stars because they saw the main characters in the same light. "Dustin is not trying to be an archetype for all fathers," Meryl told reporters on the set. "Nor am I trying to be like all women in such a situation. You have two very specific parents and a little boy. It's not necessary that you sympathize with her. It's not even necessary that you understand her. But she must be realistic. In the book, I hated her and she was no one I had ever known before. I wanted to make it a little harder for the audience to place its allegiance. Drama is conflict; the stronger the conflict, the better the story. It's obvious when we go to court that the characters are not so black and white."[6]

The courtroom scene was written to be the climax of the film. As they approached filming it, Meryl perceived Joanna's character in increasingly clearer terms. At last she had the key to the difficult task of rendering comprehensible Joanna's desertion of her husband and son for an independent search for identity. Rather than being the act of a selfish woman who callously abandons her family, then returns to disrupt their lives again, Joanna's flight was the desperate act of a woman whose self-esteem was so low that she feared she could no longer take care of herself, much less a small child.

Meryl called Benton the night before filming was to begin on the courtroom scene. She told him that if Joanna were a villain in a predictable black-hat, white-hat dispute, the climax of the film—the courtroom scene—would not be interesting. Benton asked her to rewrite the scene and promptly forgot about it. When Meryl arrived on the set with the rewrite, Benton was skeptical, seeing it as a further delay, necessitated by having to write it once again himself, and then having to soothe Meryl's offended ego. But her scene was brilliant. He later told the press, "I cut only two lines. What you see there is hers. It was as though someone set off an enormous bomb. Meryl devastated us. Because of the quality of

Meryl's performance, Joanna came out more sympathetic than she was in the book."[7]

Benton shot the scene in ten takes, including closeups, medium and long shots. "She stayed at that same level of commitment and professional intensity all day long," he remembers. "We must have shot that scene from seven in the morning until six at night, over and over again."[8] One shot was just of Hoffman's reaction to Joanna's testimony, with the entire crew focusing on him. Benton looked over at Meryl. "When it was finished," he recalls, "we turned around and there was Meryl in tears. She'd given that much all over again, just for the reaction shot. She had the same intensity as she had when she first did the scene."[9]

With Benton, Meryl's creative drive came more strongly into its own, creating a deep professional bond between them. He would later tell the press, "Meryl is one of a handful of really great actresses. There's nothing she can't do; she has no limits. She has an immense backbone of technique, but you never catch her at it."[10]

By the time that filming was finished in December, Meryl had earned the admiration not only of her director, but the entire cast and crew. Not the least of these was her demanding co-star. "She'll work twenty hours a day," Hoffman once told an interviewer. "It's like playing Billie Jean King; she is always trying to hit the perfect ball. Meryl is never at the mirror between shots, like a lot of actresses are. She's in the script, she's in your ear, saying why don't we try this or that? She has an incredible piece of working life ahead of her."[11]

The early predictions that *Kramer vs. Kramer* would be *the* movie of 1979 proved an understatement. Columbia released it just before Christmas, capitalizing on heightened feelings of family ties during that season. Despite the late release, it quickly became an overwhelming box office success.

As Meryl had told Benton, the courtroom scene was the cathartic climax of the film. Audiences were riveted as they watched Ted and Joanna bare their feelings and at last come to a mutual understanding of each other. The critics gave the film and the two stars rave reviews, particularly Meryl. Gene Siskel of the *Chicago Tribune* stated, "What all of Streep's women have in common is integrity, and a portion of that must derive from the actress herself." Stanley Kauffmann confessed that he had been "waiting for some years now for Streep to make a false move on stage or screen in widely varied characters. I'm still waiting. Meryl Streep is today's Bette Davis. Streep is first an actress, a much less mannered and self-centered actress than Davis, but with Davis' qualities of unconventional beauty and of reliance of acting as much as on stariness—the woman star who acts and does it in different roles." John Simon found her portrayal of Joanna Kramer "flawless," and *New York*'s David Denby added: "Dustin Hoffman gives the most detailed, the most affecting performance of his life . . . and Streep, avoiding all the traditional acting cliches of frustrated mother love, builds the emotion to a peak without ever raising her voice."

The reason for such universally high praise for Meryl is not difficult to understand: it lay in Meryl's determination to flesh out Joanna's character and to plumb the depths of the wrenching experience and portray all of its subtle nuances and complexities. In playing Joanna as a woman who is baffled and hurt by Ted's shortcomings and her own failures, she brought the film back into balance and provided a subtlety absent in the book. Joanna's angst and confusion rescue the film from a one-dimensional presentation obviously weighted toward Ted and Billy. Her understated suffering redeems the character of Joanna in a no-win plot; rather than a unique situation of two self-centered people, the film becomes a powerful statement on the stress that society places on contemporary marriages. Her impact upon audiences was stunning, and the public clamor in behalf of Meryl was unreserved after the film's release. It was the most significant role that she had yet done, one destined to expand her career and catapult her into star status.

As filming on *Kramer* wound down, Meryl longed to do something completely different. Developing the character of Joanna Kramer into someone that the audience could understand and have sympathy for was an exhausting process. She was approached by her longtime friend Elizabeth Swados, who had done the music for *The Cherry Orchard*, to star in her musical review *Wonderland in Concert*. It was virtually a one-woman show based upon Lewis Carroll's *Alice in Wonderland* and *Through the Looking Glass*. The part excited Meryl, but first she had to convince Benton that she could complete *Kramer* and also attend rehearsals for *Wonderland*. "It was a real job convincing these people that I could do two things at once. But to be in a vacuum with just Joanna Kramer would make for a boring Joanna. It's the theater that sustains me."[12] Reluctantly, Benton gave his approval, and Meryl began rehearsals for *Wonderland* in December.

Joseph Papp produced *Wonderland in Concert* as a Public Theater workshop of the New York Shakespeare Festival from December 27 to 29, 1978, for three performances as a musical in two acts. In it, Meryl bounces up and down, cavorting across the stage as the very embodiment of a seven-year-old girl. The pinnacle of the performance was her nonstop account of the trial of the King of Hearts, in which she plays all the characters, spinning from voice to voice in an improvised monologue. Swados would later say of her performance, "Meryl is full of surprises. With her, it's constant Christmas."[13]

Critics were charmed by Meryl's virtuoso performance. The *New York Post*'s Marilyn Stasio said, "Meryl Streep seems to have tapped some inner wellspring of eternal girlhood to come up with her glowing portrayal of the little adventurer." Mel Gussow of the *New York Times* agreed: "Miss Streep metamorphoses into Alice. . . . She sits on the stage and merrily dreams her way into the fantasy. This is a brilliant actress who has reinvented herself as a magical ageless child."

After three films and a short romp onstage as Alice, Meryl wanted a dramatic part, someone radically different from Joanna Kramer, to return to the stage in a sustained role. In January 1979, Papp provided her with that opportunity by offering her the role of Andrea in Thomas Babe's play *Taken in Marriage.*

The play centers around a wedding rehearsal in the basement of a New Hampshire church. The bride, her mother and her older sister wait for the groom's family to appear. As the afternoon wears on, the sisters begin to argue, exposing the crisscross of their lives and loves. During the most vicious of their arguments, the older sister (Andrea) delights in revealing that she has been carrying on a casual affair with the groom, whereupon the bride cancels the wedding.

Critics were enthusiastic about the all-female cast that included Kathleen Quinlan as the bride, Meryl as Andrea and Coleen Dewhurst as the mother. Meryl's interpretation captured most of the critical attention.

Andrea is airy and disconsolate; with sarcasm and aggressive-defensive behavior, she makes her unhappy way through a disordered life. As an often-married cynic, she torments her younger sister. *The New Republic*, commenting on Meryl's performance, said, "Meryl Streep, as usual, gives a mercurial star performance. Like a good novelist, Streep observes and stores the life around her, selects from her treasury of her work, then focuses the detail inward to keep it from being a mere construct. This much is true of any actor. Streep goes further. Everything — the cigarette fondling, the commenting gesture, the smiling insult — seems inevitable for the character, yet also is recognizably Streep. This dual quality, contradictory, makes the talent that stands out among talents." John Simon agreed, noting that "Streep's alabaster features convey icy disdain and mock merriment. Her voice is a bed of nails in which she sometimes lies in self-contempt."

The play itself was less favorably received. The consensus of the critics was that the outstanding cast, rather than the content of the play, make it a success. "It is not often that a dramatist is given actresses as adroit and talented as these," remarked Edith Oliver of the *New Yorker.* John Simon was even more direct: "A superb cast lends *Taken in Marriage* a trace of conviction. It is a pity that these remarkable actresses have been taken in miscarriage." Jack Kroll, *Newsweek*'s veteran drama critic, was the most complimentary about the play, principally because of Meryl's performance. "It's exciting to watch the twenty-nine-year-old Streep take more chances than any young actress around today, charging her perserved beauty with an expressive spontaneity reminiscent of the young Marlon Brando."

1978 had been a remarkable year for Meryl. She had appeared in three important films, received enthusiastic critical reviews for versatility on the stage and won an Emmy. In her private life, she had been devastated by the death of John, and been reborn in the love of Don. But 1979 would provide her with the most satisfying role of her life.

8
Reluctant Star

Because of editing and distribution problems, Michael Cimino had delayed release of *The Deer Hunter* until December 1978. It immediately caused a sensation among movie audiences and critics alike for its attempt to present a comprehensive overview of contemporary American society and the harrowing effects of war on those who fight it. The Vietnam War was still a sensitive wound in the ethos of the country. Cimino's controversial approach to that war guaranteed that the film would evoke strong emotional reactions.

Critics were divided in their interpretations of Cimino's purpose. Some believed that Cimino sought to make a patriotic film that pandered to the resurgent nationalism of the late 1970s, accompanied by disturbing overtones of racist xenophobia. Other critics regarded the film as an astute antiwar film with a sensitive feeling for time, place and blue-collar workers.

Time's Frank Rich was one of the reviewers that considered the film apolitical in perspective, a metaphor for all wars rather than the Vietnam War in particular. Rich saw the principal theme as an analysis of what happens to Americans when they experience catastrophic events for which the rituals of their daily lives leave them unprepared. The three friends are not bloodthirsty killers; rather they are ordinary foot soldiers who go off unquestioningly to fight for their country. "Cimino has attempted to embrace all the tragic contradictions of the U.S. intervention in Southeast Asia. What happens to Michael and Nick in Viet Nam is a paradigm of what happened to the U.S. Tested by an insane war, the good old American values become warped . . . a nation's manly mission turns into a self-inflicted wound."

Stanley Kauffmann feared that audiences would focus on Cimino's supposed "message" about Vietnam when, in fact, the focus was upon the three men, the impact of the war on their entrenched small-town values and how each resolves that experience in his future life. "*The Deer Hunter* is *not* about Vietnam; it's about three steelworkers, bonded in maleness," said Kauffmann, "and the differing resolutions of that experience with their futures."

Jack Kroll of *Newsweek* was another critic who saw no political

Streep (as Linda) and Robert De Niro (as Michael) in The Deer Hunter.

overtones to *The Deer Hunter*. To Kroll, the film was "nothing less than an appraisal of American life in the second half of the 20th century. *The Deer Hunter* is the first film to look at Vietnam not politically, but as the manifestation of an endemic murderousness." He saw Cimino's point to be dramatic and moral, rather than political. Therefore, although the Vietnam sequence was the shortest in the movie, "it is one of the most frightening, unbearably tense sequences ever filmed and the most violent excoriation of violence in screen history."

Pauline Kael was the most critical of what she saw as machismo and racism in the film. She found fault with Cimino's one-sided presentation of the Viet Cong as sadistic, mindless brutes, while ignoring atrocities committed by American soldiers. The suffering of the Vietnamese people was played down, showing them only as habitués of the sleazy back alleys of Saigon. "The impression a viewer gets is that if we did some bad things over there we did them ruthlessly but impersonally; the Vietcong were cruel and sadistic. The film seems to be saying that the Americans had no choice, but the V.C. enjoyed it. It's part of the narrowness of the film's vision that there is no suggestion that there ever was a sense of community among the Vietnamese which was disrupted."

Kael also saw the strong influence of James Fenimore Cooper's *Leatherstocking Tales* and Hemingway's heroes in Michael's machismo and strict sense of honor in the deer hunt. She saw the film as "the fullest screen treatment so far of the mystic bond of male comradeship. *The Deer Hunter* is a romantic adolescent boy's view of friendship, with the Vietnam War as a test of men's courage . . . with emphasis on self-reliance and will power, and their exhaltation of purity of thought—of a physical-spiritual love between men which is higher than the love between man and woman, because (presumably) it is never defiled by carnal desire." Because of the predominant machismo message, she found the film enraging because "despite its ambitiousness and scale, it has no more moral intelligence than the Eastwood action pictures."

Kauffmann also noted the strong emphasis on "male bonding" in the film, but, unlike Kael, was not offended by it. "The true subject of the film is the limitations of our society of the traditions of male mystique, the hobbling by sentimentality of a community that, after all the horror, still wants the beeriness of 'God Bless America' instead of a moral rigor and growth that might help this country."

Another theme that the critics dwelt upon was Cimino's preoccupation with ritual as a cornerstone of American society. Kroll saw the concept of ritual as *the* central theme of the film. The Russian roulette sequence is a "ritual of death," and the wedding and reception afterward is a ceremony in which "Cimino is insisting that sacraments still work where they remain rooted in a true community." Similarly, the deer hunt that follows the wedding and ends the film is "a kind of sacrament" for Michael. But Kroll viewed the hunt as a "morality that rationalizes death" and, therefore, as one of the major flaws of the film. Pauline Kael thought the evocation of ritual to be one of the few strengths of the movie. "It conveys a very distinctive love of rootedness and of the values of people whose town is their world. There's something nostalgic about this ceremonial view of ordinary American community life even as it's going on."

The scene in which the three friends are forced to play Russian roulette was a crucial element in the ritual of male courage that formed the bond between them. This scene, more than any other, divided the critics. Whereas some critics regarded the scene as contrived and disruptive to the progression of the film, Frank Rich considered it a boldly creative move by Cimino. "The roulette game becomes a metaphor for a war that blurred the lines between bravery and cruelty, friends and enemies, sanity and madness." Kauffmann viewed the torture sequence as a testing of the friends' maleness, a test to which the entire film had been building. Kroll considered it "a gut-wrenching symbol of a society committing moral suicide. This episode is the ritual of death that stands against the rituals of the life with which Cimino has structured his film."

Although discussion of Cimino's perspective and the controversial political-apolitical rendering of the film preoccupied the critics, there was widespread praise for the cast. Frank Rich commented: "There can be no quarrel about the acting. De Niro, Walken, John Savage and Meryl Streep are all top actors in extraordinary form." Stanley Kauffmann found that "the acting is always fine." Jack Kroll applauded the "superb ensemble acting from the cast. De Niro's acting is perhaps his purest yet. Christopher Walken comes strongly into his own as a film actor. As Linda, Meryl Streep, the fast-rising young American actress, gives a performance that is piercingly sweet." Vincent Canby of the *New York Times* singled out Meryl's portrayal of Linda for commendation. "Meryl Streep, who has been recognized for her fine performance on the New York stage, gives a smashing film performance as the young woman who, by tacit agreement among the friends, becomes Nick's girl but who stays around long enough to assert herself."

Pauline Kael was the most critical of the performances, not so much because they lacked quality as that they were hampered by the limitations of the script. While admiring Cimino's "talent for breadth and movement and detail," she criticized him for his inability to develop characters and reveal what is going on in a relationship, such as the Nick-Linda-Michael one. "The actors' physiognomies and intuitive byplay do most of the work of characterization; the dialogue is usually just behavorial chatter. His characters don't articulate their feelings; they're floating in a wordless, almost plotless atmosphere, and their relationships aren't sharp enough for us to feel the full range of the film's people." She was particularly disappointed in De Niro's portrayal of Michael, as much as she admired his previous work. "We have come to expect a lot from De Niro: miracles. And he delivers them. He takes the Pathfinder-Deerslayer role and gives it every flourish he can dream up. He does improvisations on nothing. But Michael, the transcendent hero, is a hollow figure." But it was to Meryl that Kael devoted most of her attention. "She doesn't do anything standard; everything seems fresh. But her role is to be the supportive woman, who suffers and endures, and it's a testament to Meryl Streep's heroic resources as a mime that she makes herself felt—she has practically no lines."

Perhaps Meryl would have found most satisfying Vincent Canby's tribute to John. "The late John Cazale makes his last film appearance a memorable one as the kind of barroom neurotic who might at any moment go seriously off his rocker."

Whatever philosophical opinion individual critics took to the film, it was undeniable that Cimino had presented the brutality of war and its effects on those that fight it in poignant, harrowing scenes. Few American films stirred up such conflicting critical reactions. Whether applauding or criticizing his efforts, reviewers admitted that he was the only director in recent years to attempt to embrace war and its consequences with such scope, one that vividly portrayed the shocking panorama of the depredations of war.

The reaction of audiences and critics to *The Deer Hunter* was officially confirmed at the 1979 Academy Awards ceremony. The film was nominated for Best Picture, Christopher Walken for Best Supporting Actor and Meryl for Best Supporting Actress. Meryl was ambivalent about the nomination. On the one hand, it was a very exciting moment; she had received an Academy Award nomination for what was only her second film. But on the other hand, it offended her feelings about competition among actors. "It's insane to have winners and losers in art," she angrily told reporters. "To say that one performance is better than another is just plain dumb. You wouldn't think of comparing two colors in a painting, would you? This blue is better than that blue?"[1]

Whatever her feelings about artists competing against each other, Meryl was present at the ceremony, nervously awaiting the announcement of the winner for Best Supporting Actress. But it was a bitter disappointment; although the film and Walken went on to win Oscars, Meryl lost out to Ellen Burstyn for her portrayal of Alice in *Alice Doesn't Live Here Anymore*. Meryl accepted her defeat philosophically, telling the press, "My dress had sweat marks under the arms, and I was glad I didn't have to get up to get the Oscar."[2]

If the Academy did not consider her performance as Linda to be of award-winning caliber, others did. She received the National Society of Film Critics Award and the Los Angeles Critics' Circle Award for Best Supporting Actress.

Meryl had always prided herself on her privacy, rigorously keeping her public and private lives separate. She and Don enjoyed prowling the streets in SoHo, going to art museums, quaint little shops and restaurants. As a stage actress, she had the best of both worlds: critical acclaim and public anonimity, unrecognized except by a small cadre of stage aficionados. But with the success of *The Deer Hunter*, when she and Don would go to museums and art galleries, they had the uncomfortable sensation of being on display along with the paintings. They could not even walk around SoHo shops, or pick over fresh fruit on sidewalk stands, without being aware of people whispering and pointing in their direction. It was the interruption of these private moments with Don that frustrated Meryl the most. That was their time together, when she wanted to put Meryl Streep the actress aside and just enjoy being Mrs. Don Gummer.

It is ironic that Meryl should be the object of so much public attention, for she has assiduously avoided the typical publicity techniques employed by unknown actresses to gain instant star recognition. "If you want to be a superstar, you have to hire a press agent and do kinky things to get into the columns," she commented bluntly. "If that is what it takes, I don't want to be a superstar. I don't want to be in the columns. Keeping my privacy is a priority."[3]

Although film offers and scripts for her consideration began to form an ever-larger pile on her desk, Meryl maintained her close ties to the New York stage. *The Village Voice* gave her an "Obie" (Off-Broadway) Award for her performance in *Wonderland in Concert*, and she was asked to emcee the Tony Awards in 1981.

Despite a promising screen career, Meryl remained ambiguous about leaving the theater for films. "Films are nice, but movies aren't going to be my life," she once told a reporter. "I can put more energy into plays, I can involve my whole body, I can open my mouth and scream."[4]

In the spring of 1979, Meryl began talking to Joe Papp about her dream of putting together a traveling repertory company to perform Shakespeare around the country. He encouraged her to solicit other actors; eventually, she enlisted Al Pacino, Rosemary Harris, Jon Voight, Marybeth Hurt and Dustin Hoffman, among others. As the project began to take form, Meryl's enthusiasm increased. "An actor would do Hamlet on one night and Polonius the next," she told a reporter. "I could do Gertrude and Ophelia. And we could film it."[5] But Papp's commitments prevented any follow-through on the plan. She was deeply disappointed, but refused to give up the idea completely; it was just a priority that would have to wait.

"Maybe when we're all fifty-five we can take a year off and not worry about what the other person is doing behind one's back. It would be wonderful to look back twenty years from now and say, 'I was with the troupe in 1980.' It would be like saying, 'I was with the Group Theater' or 'I was with Ellis Robb and Rosemary Harris at the Association of Producing Artists' or 'I was on tour with Katherine Cornell.'"[6]

Meryl had now reached a point in her career where she no longer felt compelled to accept any stage or screen offer that came her way; she could afford to be more selective in her choice of roles. She still wanted to do stage tragedy and film comedy, perhaps some Shakespeare or another musical. She had briefly considered the role of Eva Peron in the musical *Evita*, and sent out feelers through her agent, but the role went to Patti LaPone.

The Gummers settled into a routine of quiet domesticity. Meryl would wade through the pile of scripts on her desk, carefully weighing the projects and granting interviews while Don worked on his sculpture in the studio in the front of their loft apartment.

Meryl's thoughts increasingly turned to starting a family. "My work has been very important because if you want a career, I feel that you have to build a foundation in your twenties. But we wanted to have a child because we felt that not enough people in our circle of friends were having children. Friends of mine from college, who are very accomplished, were all delaying children until they are older, because of their careers."[7] On November 13, 1979, Meryl gave birth to Henry Wolfe Gummer, named for her father in the Streep tradition. But young Henry soon became known as "Gippy" to his proud parents.

Revelling in the joys of motherhood, Meryl told reporters, "There was nothing to it. Don was with me and the baby right after it was born. It seemed the most natural thing in the world. This baby is an affirmative commitment in pretty desperate times. It's the biggest thing that's ever happened to me."[8]

Meryl insisted on being a totally involved mother. Even in breaks of photo sessions, she would stop to breast-feed Henry or change his diapers during interviews. At these times, she would speak radiantly about Henry. "Having a baby is the greatest thing ever! I hate this myth that your life is taken over, destroyed by a kid."[9] When asked the inevitable question about what having a child would do to her career, Meryl quickly asserted that motherhood was her primary role in life. "Yes, my life is irrevocably changed, but the baby is an injection of unexpected joy. My husband and I compete for the right to take care of him. Sometimes when he's sleeping peacefully at night, we talk about waking him up so we can go comfort him."[10]

Now that she had a baby, Meryl began to view their neighborhood with misgivings; it was one thing to putter around it with just Don, but with a baby, she now saw it differently. "Since I had Henry, I've begun to think that SoHo is ugly. In the past, I never noticed—I just thought of the wonderful people inside the buildings. But with a kid, there's no place to go. And the auto exhausts are at just the same height as a baby carriage."[11]

She and Don bought a 95-acre wooded area on a mountaintop in Duchess County, New York. They left the original cottage and one of the outbuildings, converting the other into a studio for Don. This became their refuge when the pressures of New York became too much for them. They would retreat to it more and more frequently as the hoopla surrounding the success of *Kramer vs. Kramer* intensified.

9
The Year of Streep

A number of prestigious awards descended upon Meryl in 1980. The Los Angeles Film Critics' Circle and the New York Film Critics' Circle cited her for her performance in *The Seduction of Joe Tynan* and *Kramer vs. Kramer*. Harvard's Hasty Pudding Club chose her as its Woman of the Year, and she received the Golden Globe Award for Best Motion Picture Actress in 1979.

Meryl capped off the year of triumph at the fifty-second annual Academy Awards ceremony on April 15, 1980. Despite her previous statements about the absurdity of awards for individual roles between actors and actresses, Meryl appeared at the ceremony with all the typical nervousness of nominees. New York governor Hugh Carey's Office for Motion Picture and Television Development, elated over the fact that twenty-five percent of the nominees were from New York, gave a party on April 8 for all New York nominees at the Tavern on the Green. Most prominent among the guests were Meryl (*Kramer vs. Kramer*), Robert De Niro (*Raging Bull*), Melvyn Douglas (*Being There*), Justin Henry (*Kramer vs. Kramer*) and Barbara Barrie (*Breaking Away*).

Arriving at the Los Angeles airport on the night before the ceremony, Meryl crossed her fingers as she nervously fielded reporters' questions. Shouting about the tumult, she told them, "I'm trying to hear your questions over my heartbeat."[1] Still on New York time, she arose at 6:00 a.m. and spent the day in her suite in the Beverly Hills Hotel with Don and Henry, waiting for the limousine that would take her to the ceremony at the Dorothy Chandler Pavilion. "It feels like limbo land here," she told reporters. "There's nothing to do except wait."[2] As she sought to calm her frayed nerves, her mind was in turmoil. Would the other awards prove to be a prelude to the best-known of them all, or end in disappointment?

Meryl was disappointed that her role in *Kramer vs. Kramer* was considered a supporting role, and thus placed her in the category of a nominee for Best Supporting Actress rather than Best Actress, but this year's ceremony would not be a repeat of 1978, when she lost out to Ellen Burstyn. After her name was announced as the winner of the Best Supporting category, she ran to the podium, momentarily forgetting the dignified acceptance speech that she had prepared, blurting out, "Holy Mack-erel!"

Every Oscar awards ceremony has its favorite story, but surely Meryl's must rank as one of the most memorable. While the ceremonies were still going on, a female reporter went into the ladies' room, only to reemerge shouting, "Hey, someone left an Oscar in here." Meryl rushed backstage to claim it, horrified that she had left the coveted statue in a stall. "Oh, my God," she screamed. "How could I have done that? It shows how nervous I really am."[3]

The publicity surrounding the Oscar made a profound impact on Meryl's career, but proved disruptive to her private life. She was deluged with requests for interviews. Because of the favorable critical and audience reception to *The Seduction of Joe Tynan, Manhattan* and *Kramer vs. Kramer*, the press began referring to 1979 as "The Year of Streep." At one point, her photograph was on the cover of *Time, Newsweek, Rolling Stone* and the *New York Times Magazine* simultaneously.

If the intrusions into her private life had been disruptive before, they now became a nightmare to Meryl. She eventually refused all interviews for several months. "I think that the notion that you owe it to your public is kind of odd. Nobody else does that except elected officials, and I'm not elected. I feel great responsibility towards what I do, to my work and to making *that* communication as good as I can; but outside of that, I don't feel I owe anybody anything. And it seems bizarre to think that I have to share the few private moments I have with other people. I share many private moments with other people on screen or onstage, and I think that's enough."[4]

The film offers descended úpon her, but she insisted on reading each and carefully selecting just the right one. She had reached a point in her career where she did not feel compelled to accept any offer that came along. What bothered her most of all were the requests for photo sessions and interviews that took her away from Gippy. She and Don recognized that with their two hectic careers, they were going to have to compromise their belief in being totally involved parents, and they hired a nanny for Henry.

One film offer intrigued her more than the others. United Artists had bought the rights to John Fowles' intricate novel *The French Lieutenant's Woman*, and hired Karel Reisz to direct it. Reisz had seen Meryl's work in *Kramer* and wanted her for the lead. Filming was scheduled to begin in June. At last, Meryl was being offered the lead in an important film; it eased the disappointment in not being considered the leading lady in *Kramer*.

Don was busy at work on a gigantic piece to go in the United Nations Plaza, and he was hurrying so that he and Gippy could accompany Meryl to London in June. May was a month of disorganized panic as they packed for the trip. But by the end of the month, Don had finished the sculpture, and they left for London, where they spent a week in an apartment in Kensington Gardens before leaving for Lyme Regis and the start of the filming schedule.

The French Lieutenant's Woman is a moody, romantic tableau set in mid-nineteenth-century Lyme Regis, a small English seacoast town in Dorset. It involves a lusty, fallen Victorian heroine who defies convention and ruins her life and that of her lover in a doomed fixation about a previous lover who jilted her. The plot is a multi-leveled romance in which two lovers experience passion and despair. Charles Smithson (Jeremy Irons) is a gentleman archaeologist who has come to Lyme Regis to study fossils in the area. As he walks along the windswept jetty with his fiancée, Ernestina (Lynsey Baxter), he sees a mysterious, cloaked figure at the end, seemingly about to be swept into the sea. As he rushes out to warn her, he is transfixed by the haunted, sorrowful look on her face and retreats, confused. She is Sarah Woodruff (Meryl), an ex-governess ostracized in the community for having an affair with a French naval officer. She skulks around the village in silent guilt, but with a fierce pride that will not ask forgiveness. She goes to the jetty every day, futilely waiting for her lover who will never return.

At this point, the camera pans back and the audience sees that it is a movie set. Two actors, Anna (Meryl) and Mike (Irons), are in a movie in which they portray Charles and Sarah. The film shifts back and forth between the story of the two lovers, and the modern story of the love affair between Mike and Anna. The viewer quickly perceives that, unlike the tempestuous love affair between Charles and Sarah, the tryst of Mike and Anna is a shallow dalliance that will not survive the filming.

The setting returns to Lyme Regis in 1867. Charles is fascinated by Sarah's mysteriousness and pursues her until she confesses her love affair with the naval officer. He cannot decide whether she is mad or just an independent woman ahead of her time, but he cannot resist her. He forsakes his friends, abandons his fiancée, and ruins his reputation and career in pursuit of Sarah. The experience is tortuous for Charles, but he is hopelessly in the throes of an obsession. He pours out his frustration to a psychologist friend (Leo McKern), but can find no solace in the advice to return to his fiancée and forget Sarah.

In one passion-filled night, Charles sleeps with Sarah. He awakes to find that Sarah is gone. The film presents three separate endings to the audience. In one, Charles is reunited with Sarah after a three-year separation, and they tenderly fall in love again. In the second, they are also reunited, but Charles is callous and unfeeling when he finds Sarah again. In the third ending, the scene returns to the contemporary love story of Mike and Anna. Mike can no longer distinguish between the fictional character he is portraying and the reality of the movie set. At a cast party after the last scene is filmed, Anna callously prepares to leave without saying goodbye. Charles rushes after the retreating car shouting, "Sarah!"

Streep (as Sarah Woodruff) and Jeremy Irons (as Charles Smithson) in an intense dramatic scene from The French Lieutenant's Woman.

Despite the Oscar and the plaudits of 1979, Meryl was not yet "bankable," that is, a star whose very name would attract producers and guarantee a box-office bonanza. To do that, she needed a starring role in an important film. But because of the Oscar, she had come to the attention of Reisz and now had the opportunity to create a memorable role that would utilize all of her considerable talents and classical stage training. If she could bring to life all of the complex contradictions of Sarah's persona, there would be no more supporting roles and bit parts. Until now, she had played vulnerable modern women; she was tired of playing contemporary women. The role of Sarah Woodruff gave her the opportunity to reach into the past and bring to life a character from another era.

But the film was a very difficult one to bring to the screen. The project had been a thorny problem for a dozen producers since the book was published in 1969. Several studios had optioned it, but all had failed to adequately encompass the plot's labyrinth of subtle meanings into a manageable script. Finally, United Artists hired Harold Pinter to write an innovative screenplay that would interweave the cunning conundrum of the novel with a spellbinding story.

Although the riddle of a workable script had been solved, the film continued to be beset with problems. In addition to the numerous unsuccessful attempts of extremely talented screenwriters to bring it to the screen, there was a steady stream of directors. Fred Zinnemann, Mike Nichols and Franklin Schaeffer had all been hired as directors and failed. Only Reisz had the breadth of vision to successfully cope with the dilemma of Fowles' metaphysical ruminations and the torrid romantic plot of the novel. Rumors abounded that Reisz had sought to interest a number of prominent actresses in the lead role. Reisz himself insisted that he only had Meryl in mind to play the tempestuous Sarah. He was only too glad to sign Meryl for the part; he had seen her in *The Deer Hunter* and *Kramer vs. Kramer*, and thought she would bring just the right essence of volatility to the difficult role of Sarah, the "scarlet woman of Lyme Regis."

Don and Gippy had been able to stay with Meryl for the first month of filming, but in July Don had to return to New York for a one-man show. Although Gippy remained with Meryl in Lyme Regis, Meryl found the separation from Don difficult. "I felt so cut off," she recalls. "The phone bill for five weeks in Lyme Regis was $500."[5]

In that moody, windswept setting, Meryl again plunged into her rigorous routine of preparation, endlessly reading Fowles' novel to immerse herself into the difficult task of moulding Sarah's character. She had serious doubts about her ability to bring Sarah effectively to life. Perhaps the most difficult thing Meryl had to do in creating Sarah's persona was to recreate the high level of good manners and propriety of the era even while she showed the internal fire that threatened to consume Sarah. "I realized the passions run so high *because* they were so repressed. That's a difficult thing to capture on screen."[6]

If Meryl believed that Reisz had conceived of her as Sarah from the start, she was not so convinced about author John Fowles, who served as technical advisor on the film. She had heard gossip that Fowles had wanted an English actress for the part, preferably Vanessa Redgrave. In fact, Fowles had no preconceptions concerning the actress to portray Sarah, other than her "essence," which Meryl fulfilled to his highest expectations.

Meryl was so nervous about Fowles' reaction to her interpretation of Sarah that she initially avoided him on the set, much to Fowles' frustration. "She was very shy about me," he recalled. "When I'd appear on the set, she'd hide. She had some extraordinary notion that I didn't want an American actress. But there's no English actress of her age group who could have done it."[7] Ironically, Fowles preferred an American actress to portray Sarah, believing that the rebellion and striving for freedom necessary in her character required an American rather than English focus. Meryl was so intent on doing justice to the complex Sarah that she constantly reread the book between scenes, a devotion to the original intent that touched Fowles deeply.

As much as he wanted Meryl for the role, Reisz worried that she would
be unable to master the complexity of nineteenth century English speech
and inflection and considered dubbing her lines. Meryl was horrified; it
was counter to everything that she believed in terms of creating the reality
necessary to make Sarah come alive for the audience. She read aloud from
the King James version of the Bible and novels by Jane Austen and George
Eliot to perfect her accent and hired a voice coach. She became so pro-
ficient that she completely fooled a close friend in one of her transatlantic
telephone calls to New York.

In order to be faithful to the Sarah presented in the novel, a sensuous,
defiant woman, Meryl dyed her hair coppery red to convey illicit passion.
She had considered using tinted contact lenses for Sarah's bewitching
green eyes, but the first rushes showed her eyes green without the lenses.

Meryl appeared calm and confident in creating both Sarah's physical
and psychological persona, but it was a facade that she maintained to
disguise her anxiety. One source of that anxiety was the enormous responsibility of the double role. Additionally, as the only American in the cast,
Meryl worried that the English cast would resent her presumption in portraying an English woman. "I felt like an outcast," she confessed later. "I
felt like an American girl playing the part of an English woman and
pariah."[8] But the cast was impressed by her precision in perfecting the
difficult dialect and her thoroughness in researching her role, and they
were friendly.

Meryl was particularly interested in capturing a certain look in Sarah's
eyes, an intelligence and stubborn determination to be what she was, and
a spirited independence that was willing to suffer ostracism as the price of
her freedom and avant-garde behavior. Many of the characteristics of Sarah
Woodruff, as described in the novel, meshed well with the quirky mannerisms that critics had come to associate with Meryl in diverse roles.
Meryl developed a subtle blend of the character from the book and her own
perceptions of Sarah until the character and the actress became blurred
in distinction. Fowles was amazed at how Meryl gave an uncannily exact
translation of the description into screen life. In the book, Sarah was
described as having an "over-small" voice, with pauses between clipped,
tentative sentences. Fowles was impressed with how Meryl's creation of
the film character did precise and breathtaking justice to his book and the
character of Sarah.

This blurring of screen persona and actor became the basis of solving
one of the film's most vexing problems. What had doomed all previous
scripts was trying to incorporate this phenomenon, which Fowles dealt
with at length in the book. It was Pinter and Reisz that supplied the in-
genious solution: a movie-within-a-movie. Meryl was not only to portray
Sarah, but also Anna, the woman playing Sarah in the film, just as Jeremy
Irons had to play the dual role of Charles/Mike. In this manner, Reisz was

able to deal at length with the phenomenon of persona and actor blurring as the twin love affairs are portrayed. By this device, the film became a remarkable shifting of tenses and tensions as the action shifts from the Victorian story to the modern love affair between the two contemporary actors.

The film-within-a-film device delighted Meryl; it allowed her to pursue her personal interest in the dilemma common to many actors, the difficulty of separating oneself from one's screen role. As the scenes shifted back and forth between Sarah and Anna, Meryl had to develop two radically different personalities: the aloof, urbane, almost frighteningly controlled Anna, and the wild, unpredictable Sarah. Even her two faces were as different as the two personalities.

Meryl portrayed Sarah as a strange, sensual beauty tormented by a tragic fate. But as Anna, she was detached, professional, having a casual location love affair with Mike, who is desperately in love with her. The three endings that Reisz gave the film were designed to intensify the dichotomy between actor and film persona. Anna had no difficulty in keeping the two separate, but in the third ending, Mike tries to find Anna at the cast party after filming is finished, and calls out "Sarah" after Anna's retreating car; he is unable to distinguish between his film lover and his modern one. Fowles himself suggested that one line, and it worked magnificently.

As in *The Deer Hunter* and *Kramer vs. Kramer*, Meryl formed a fast friendship with her co-star, Jeremy Irons. Whereas Meryl quickly perceived Sarah and Anna's personalities, drawing upon her exacting attention to detail to draw up the emotions needed to allow the sexual and intellectual demands of the twin roles to flow through the power of her acting, Irons had serious doubts as to his ability to create distinctly different personas for Charles and Mike. This was Irons' first screen role after a promising career on the London stage. Having gone through the same process herself, Meryl continually bolstered Irons' confidence and helped him work out the two difficult parts.

The film is one of stormy onset of passion from the first scene where Charles is so struck by the sensual, haunted expression on Sarah's face. But there are two exceptionally powerful scenes in the movie that underscore the theme of smouldering desire. In one, Sarah stands at a mirror, one hand clutching the other as she furiously sketches a self-portrait of "the mad woman of Lyme Regis." The audience is unable to tell whether Sarah is mad or merely rehearsing an elaborate charade in which she will reveal the details of her love affair with the French naval officer. Meryl sought to portray Sarah as if her sanity were constantly in doubt, and she succeeds brilliantly in this unspoken scene in which Sarah's feverish preparations could be either the machinations of a psychotic personality or the calculated effects of a willful, self-centered woman.

The other scene is a dramatically intense one on the cliff above Lyme Regis where Sarah makes her confession to Charles. It is a long, nine-minute monologue that, if not handled with delicacy, could sound flat and theatrical, destroying the tension and tempo of the scene. For the scene, Meryl wore unflattering makeup, conveying weather-roughened features and red eyes to underscore her haunted soul. Her monologue is a blend of fact and fiction, to the point that neither Charles nor the audience is sure that the seduction ever took place.

It was a beautifully acted scene, very sensual, in which Meryl's expression subtly changes with each piece of information that Sarah gives to Charles about the seduction. In it, Meryl proved herself to be a marvelously expressive actress who fills her eyes and speech with emotions ranging from utter desolation to fiery pride. She appears to be sorting through a myriad of nuances before selecting one—just the right one—for that precise moment.

As Sarah describes the officer's attentions, she has a girlish, virginal smile; the smile slowly fades as she shyly describes how the sailor plied her with wine, only to be replaced by an angry denial that she acted from any other motive than her own desires. Sarah then begins to undo her hair, letting it fall around her shoulders, a seemingly calculated effect to deliberately arouse Charles under the guise of describing the seduction. Sarah's description of the scene reaches a peak of intensity and fervor until she finally screams out, "I am the French Lieutenant's . . . whore!"

The cliff scene was the most demanding of Meryl because of the sustained monologue. It had to be interesting and real, not like a stage piece. It took all day to film, much like the courtroom scene in *Kramer vs. Kramer*, but, as Meryl admitted later, "the effort was treble."[9]

All through the five weeks at Lyme Regis, Meryl had been a source of succor, first to Irons, then to Reisz, when either expressed any misgivings about the film's progress. It was only at the end of the filming schedule that Meryl allowed any self-doubts to arise in her own mind. "Watching the film, I couldn't help wishing I was more beautiful. I really wish I was the kind of actress who could have just stood there and said it all."[10]

If Meryl had any doubts about the quality of her performance, no one else did. Meryl had captivated the entire cast and crew. Pinter was ecstatic over her interpretation of Sarah. "Meryl's superb. She is quite a remarkable actress with vivacious and singular vibrations."[11] Karel Reisz echoed Pinter's praises, adding: "Meryl is the most extraordinary mixture of the emotional and intuitive. Sarah is one of those parts that requires flights of the imagination that are steep and complex. Meryl prepares things on the day of shooting, then it all evaporates. She throws herself into the wind and she lets it take her."[12]

The French Lieutenant's Woman received mixed critical reviews upon its release in September 1981. Critical commentary was divided between those that were offended by the confusing cutting back and forth from the Victorian lovers to those in the twentieth century, and those that praised the film for its daring and the irony and paradox in the characters.

Vincent Canby of the *New York Times* enthused: "'The French Lieutenant's Woman' is an astonishingly beautiful film, acted to the hilt by Meryl Streep. Miss Streep has never looked more beautiful nor has she been more in command of her talent." He also had unreserved praise for Jeremy Irons. "Mr. Irons is so completely convincing as the Victorian lover who is ahead of his time, but who finds, ultimately, that he still has a long way to go."

Time's Richard Corliss was less impressed with the quality of the film than with Meryl's performance. "This is the first film that depends crucially on her to light a sexual-intellectual flame, and she draws on her compassion, intelligence, wit — and considerable resources of mystery — to create two utterly different characters. but the creation might have remained stillborn without the contribution of Meryl Streep. This Sarah, this Anna, this warring family of sirens demands an incandescent star. With this performance, Streep . . . provides a new life to a cinema starved for shining stars."

Corliss was not the only reviewer to focus upon Meryl's solemn face and expressive eyes in creating the tempestuous Sarah. Many recognized in her portrayal of Sarah the combination of desire and anguished pain. Her Sarah is a woman of seething, repressed desire, an iconoclast who was an outcast from her society, a mysterious femme fatale who uses all her considerable charm to deceive the hapless Charles. Of Meryl's performance, David Ansen said, "The transition from the Victorian to the modern is embodied in the elusive figure of Sarah, whose stubborn, possibly deranged concept of freedom sets her apart from her times. Meryl Streep's fascinating performance makes clear that [Sarah] is inventing her role in life as she goes along. Streep is not an ingratiating performer. . . . With her severe, almost witchlike beauty, her darting, almost bashful presence, she plays a kind of hide-and-seek with the camera, preferring challenge to charm."

David Denby of *New York* magazine was also charmed by Meryl's performance. "As Sarah Woodruff, the genteel governess jilted by the mysterious Frenchman, Meryl Streep presents a persona that is practically a movie in itself—pale, passionate, with wildly darting greenish eyes, a small frightened mouth, and suggestions of sensual abandon."

Although Pauline Kael complimented Meryl as an accomplished technician, she remained disenchanted with her performance as Sarah. "Meryl Streep gives an immaculate, technically accomplished performance, but she isn't mysterious. She's pallid and rather glacial. . . . There's no passion, and not even any special stress. Meryl Streep's technique doesn't add up to anything. We're not fascinated by Sarah, she's so distanced from us that all we can do is observe how meticulous Streep — and everything else about the movie — is." She was not completely negative regarding Meryl's attempts to make Sarah a mysterious, alluring heroine, commenting that "Meryl Streep has a few moments that register." One of these was the very moving scene when Sarah, in a moment of retrospection, sketches herself. But, overall, she felt that Meryl missed the mark in trying to create the complex persona of Sarah. "Streep seems to be examining her performance while she gives it."

Judith Crist, writing for the *Saturday Review*, picked up a theme that troubled a number of critics: the juxtaposition of the Victorian and modern love stories. "The flip-flop to modern sequences, which serves to replace the omniscient author with the movie-within-a-movie . . . does not work." She found the solution, while daring, to be "mechanical and contrived, with the two endings confusing." Continuing this theme, Richard Corliss judged the parallel stories to be annoying and intrusive to the plot. "What in the book passes for philosophical reflection becomes show-business wit in the movie."

David Ansen of *Newsweek*, however, was not offended by the dual story device, which he believed stimulated the audience by the difference in the two courtships, one casual and modern, the other one of repressed sexuality. To Ansen, it was "an enormously clever tour de force, dexterously shuffling postmodern self-consciousness into a popular novel . . . [the device] feels successful. The beauty of the solution is in its boldness." Rex Reed, by contrast, thought the device a complete failure. "The film-within-a-film device allows ironic contrasts and similarities between the morality of two different eras, but it's an annoying conceit that destroys the illusion of the book and irritates the audience."

Meryl's attempt to make Sarah's state of mind ambiguous was another aspect of the film that divided most critics. The scene that was intended to project this ambiguity, the one on the cliff where Sarah describes her seduction to Charles, failed to impress Pauline Kael, who found it "with no passion, not even any special stress . . . so there was no weight in the movie. Since she's [Sarah] not especially fascinating, it's hardly an urgent issue. You don't know what happened, and you don't care." Richard Corliss, on the other hand, believed that Meryl had skillfully brought to life the inner complexities of Sarah's personality. "By keeping her voice calm, quiet, governessy, Streep makes Sarah thoroughly ambiguous and enigmatic." Rex Reed, who generally viewed Meryl's performance unfavorably, reluctantly concluded that "Streep's Sarah is a mysterious, sullen sensualist."

It remained for George Gastoer, in the prestigious *Film Comment*, to pronounce the final word on both the film and Meryl's performance. "'The French Lieutenant's Woman' is an exceptional film that is bound to become a kind of classic in literature-to-film adaptation. Crucial to the success of the project was the casting of Meryl Streep. Meryl Streep in both roles is a consummate actress who retains the integrity of her feminine mystery. The beauty of the performances brings us immediately into the story. One of the most impressive adaptations of a novel in recent memory and easily one of the best movies of the year."

Returning to New York, Meryl sought to revive her interest in a traveling repertory company and contacted Joseph Papp. By this time, however, Papp's conception had evolved into a series of plays with an ensemble of the leading Broadway and Hollywood actors and actresses. The troupe would include, in all, about twenty-five actors. He wanted to revive the theater and reverse the trend where the best stage actors were lured away to films, or at least create an atmosphere that would encourage film actors to return to the stage periodically. The new repertory company was scheduled to go into rehearsals January 1981 and spend three months in performances, closing in April. Papp intended to present three plays in repertory, with Meryl and Robert De Niro appearing in all three. As Papp outlined the plan to Meryl, the only definite play he had was Chekhov's *The Three Sisters*, where she would once again be directed by the controversial Andre Serban. Unfortunately, the idea did not come to fruition, perhaps because the project would cost an estimated $11.4 million, and Papp assessed the expected box-office revenues to amount to no more than $225,000 at best.

The only play to come out of the aborted Papp repertory company was a revival of Elizabeth Swados' *Wonderland in Concert*, under the title *Alice in Concert*, as part of the New York Shakespeare Festival for the 1980–1981 season. Rehearsals began on November 4, 1980, and the play opened on December 9 for a six-week run. It was eventually taped by NBC-TV for a prime-time special.

Critics panned the show, but raved about Meryl's performance. "There is only one wonder in 'Alice in Concert,'" said the review in the *New York Times*, "and it goes by the name of Meryl Streep. Maybe it's gratuitous to rave about this amazing actress at this late date, but what else is there to do? One leaves the Public (Theater) owing this star a considerable debt. Imagine 'Alice' without her, and it's hard to picture the show at all."

Although the reviews gave passing notice to the ten supporting characters that had been added since Meryl's one-woman show, the attention was rightly focused on Meryl. As in the workshop two years before, Meryl transformed herself into the dreamy Alice, dressed in blue overalls and a white turtleneck, on a cramped stage surrounded by thirty-five musicians. Particularly affecting was the scene when Meryl seems to take leave of gravity as she falls through the rabbit hole. Critics found another lovely moment when she wakes from a nap and looks into a spotlight to "brush her flowing hair, her eyes dewy and face so pure that she truly appears to have been reborn as a young girl."

Time's Frank Rich was enamored with what he termed "her fascinating display of technique. As, for example, when she, successively, becomes a giggly nymphet, a spoiled brat and a lost, teary-eyed waif. In a tour de force she adds other characters to her repertory in addition to playing Alice. A particularly touching effect was her portrayal as the dowager White Queen and her humorous impersonation of Humpty Dumpty, which she accomplished solely by affecting a forlorn, basso profundo voice, again utilizing her amazing vocal range."

But Rich was distinctly unimpressed with Elizabeth Swados' "toneless music," which included thirty-six songs. "Miss Swados has ostensibly been working on this score for seven years—and that may be the problem. You're not going to leave the theater humming any melodies. There are no laughs here beyond those provided by the antics of Miss Streep. At least Miss Streep, God bless her, insists on going her own merry way."

In the spring of 1981, Meryl began filming a thriller written and directed by Robert Benton entitled *Stab!* Sam Rice (Roy Scheider) is a psychiatrist whose patient, George Bynum (Josef Sommer), is murdered. Bynum had been the curator of antiquities at Crispin's, a large auction house. Bynum had described his affair with a woman at the auction house in such graphic detail that Rice finds himself interested, particularly when Bynum reveals that she had killed a man several years ago. The day after the murder, a strikingly beautiful Brooke Reynolds (Meryl) comes to Rice's office to return the wristwatch that Bynum had left in her apartment. Rice, who is half in love with Brooke already from Bynum's conversations, reads back through his notes to see if Brooke, or whoever, could be the murderer from clues in Bynum's erotic ramblings of other affairs.

Rice and Brooke continue to meet and quickly fall in love. Now Rice is in a quandary; he is not sure that Brooke is the killer, but there is a dark secret in her past and, now that he is love with her, he can no longer maintain the necessary objectivity of a clinical psychiatrist. He enlists the aid of his mother, Grace Rice (Jessica Tandy), who is also a psychiatrist. One thing that particularly concerns Rice is that Brooke, under her surface sophisticated beauty, may be a psychotic—and Rice himself may be her next victim. Police detective Joe Vitucci (Joe Grifasi) is convinced that Brooke is the killer and pressures Rice to reveal the confidential notes of Bynum's sessions. Rice, however, becomes more and more convinced that Brooke is innocent; but, if she is not the killer, then who is? He begins to suspect that he is being stalked by someone, and races to discover the identity of the true killer before he becomes the next victim.

Brooke retreats to her father's remote Long Island estate to escape the pressure from Rice, the police and the press. Rice pursues her there after reading about a revealing dream sequence that Bynum once conveyed to him. In the meantime, Vitucci calls upon another woman, Gail Phillips (Sara Botsford), who also works at Crispin's. While Vitucci waits for Phillips, he is murdered by an unseen assailant.

The climax of the film occurs when Sam confronts Brooke on a high balcony at the house. He tells her about the dream that Bynum had, which was based on a story Brooke had once told him in bed. In an emotionally taut scene, Brooke confesses that she accidentally killed her father when he was trying to molest her; in the struggle on a balcony in a Rome hotel, her father had toppled backward over the railing.

Rice suddenly realizes who the murderer is. He tells Brooke to remain at the house while he goes for the police. As he enters the car, he is attacked by a knife-wielding assailant. Brooke, hearing something outside, opens the door, only to be confronted by a wild-eyed Gail Phillips. As Phillips pursues Brooke through the house, she screams out her hatred of Brooke and Bynum, who had jilted her for Brooke. Phillips corners Brooke on the same balcony where Sam had plied the truth out of Brooke. As Phillips is about to stab Brooke, she is distracted by a wounded Rice at the door. In turning, Phillips loses her footing and plunges off the balcony and down the cliff.

Benton had been working on the script periodically for four years, constantly changing the plot in his attempt to make the film a homage to Alfred Hitchcock. Meryl enjoyed the opportunity to work with Benton again, and continued to make plot changes and contribute to the revision of the script, as she had done in *Kramer vs. Kramer*. "It started as a homage to Hitchcock," she told the press, "but Benton wanted to deepen it, and I helped him a little. I would suggest things to him from my own experiences, my own prejudices, and then Benton would work them into the script."[13] Meryl was also pleased to work with her co-star Roy Scheider. "He has that special Cary Grant quality—adding an element of class to the circumstances."[14]

But the magic combination of Benton-Streep did not work, as it had in *Kramer*. There were innumerable problems connected with the project because of delays in filming schedules and constant script rewrites. The accumulations of problems on the set had their effect on Meryl and cast a pall over the entire cast and crew. In one scene, Meryl displayed a rare moment of artistic pique. "I just couldn't get a scene right. The dialogue seemed false. I got madder and madder because I knew the answer lay within me, but I couldn't wrestle it up. I sulked all day—something I never did before. There's a lot of tension toward the end of a film, because the answers *have* to be there."[15] Benton was so dissatisfied with the film that he decided to delay release indefinitely to do extensive editing.

The French Lieutenant's Woman was not nominated for Best Picture. It was beaten out by an unusually large field of strong contenders: *Atlantic City, Chariots of Fire, On Golden Pond, Raiders of the Lost Ark* and *Reds.* It was, however, nominated for several lesser awards: Best Screenplay Based on Material from Another Medium, Best Art Direction, and Best Film Editing (although it did not win in any of these categories). Meryl was nominated for Best Actress for her portrayal of Sarah Woodruff, along with Katharine Hepburn (*On Golden Pond*), Diane Keaton (*Reds*), Marsha Mason (*Only When I Laugh*) and Susan Sarandon (*Atlantic City*). To no one's surprise, Katherine Hepburn won for her excellent performance in *On Golden Pond*.

Even if she had won, the Oscar would not have diminished Meryl's attitude toward competition that had made her life at Yale so difficult. And now that she had several good films to her credit, there was the added pressure of critics comparing her most recent work to her previous films. "I'm not comfortable competing with myself," she said shortly after the Academy Awards ceremony. "When I was in the country one weekend, I swam a mile and my husband Don lent me a waterproof watch so I could time myself—I was traumatized halfway through—swimming much more slowly than usual. I get extraordinarily nervous in any arena with a sports-like feeling."[16]

Her intense dislike of competition was evidenced when she was asked to preside at the 1981 Tony Awards. Although an experienced and accomplished actress who had often memorized pages of dialogue with no trouble, she panicked. "I'd memorized my speech," she recalls, "but at the last minute I decided to make it easier on myself by reading from the teleprompter. Well, the medium broke down and I thought I'd *die*."[17]

Meryl's nervousness in front of crowds did not prevent her from becoming a highly visible supporter of controversial issues. The cause most dear to her heart is nuclear disarmament. When asked why she would speak before large crowds when it so obviously frightened her, Meryl replied, "I figure that nuclear disarmament is the only thing worth giving up a bit of my privacy for. When I wake up in the dead of night to get Henry a glass of water, I realize that issues such as disarmament, equal rights, looking out for the disadvantaged, all are about him. I don't want to get too busy to care."[18]

Motherhood has always been Meryl's most important role, one which takes precedence even over her devotion to her craft. "I wasn't prepared for the enormous emotion—the love," she confesses. "It's really overwhelming. Motherhood is a great thing, easier and more fun than anyone told me. I definitely believe in it." At the time of those remarks, Meryl was contemplating having another child someday, but said she would "put off a decision on that for a while."[19]

As Henry grew older, Meryl began to think about what being the son of an actress would do to him, and what burdens he would have to face as he came to realize that his mother was a celebrity. The story of children of movie stars is often a traumatic one, where they lose all sense of their own identity, having to adjust to living life in a goldfish bowl of publicity, and feeling the pressure of obligation to live up to the reputation of a famous parent.

Meryl was determined that would not happen to little Henry. "I think that's one of the hardest things in the world. That's why I want to shield him. When I was a little kid, I was the star in my household. That's how it should be for all little kids. When you're a little kid, you should be the light of the house.

"Don has very strong feelings about that, too. We have a wonderful poster of me, and I was thinking of hanging it in Henry's room. Then I realized that would be a mistake. The last thing Henry needs is me peering down at him day and night. He has to be able to shut the door and get away from Mommy."[20]

Of course, Meryl also has the concerns universal to all mothers everywhere, that have nothing to do with fame. "I want to teach him 'no' so he won't walk into traffic. But also 'yes' so he'll have the gift of enjoying life. And I'd like to teach him concern for others."[21]

She, Don and Henry moved out of the loft in Tribeca, an artists' section of Manhattan, to an unpretentious but larger loft in Little Italy where they would be less under public scrutiny. Meryl spent her days as a housewife and mother, being a twenty-four-hour companion to Don and Henry. She continued to get scripts from her agent, Sam Cohn, to consider. Unlike many actresses, Meryl took her time with each script, insisting on reading not only her part, but the entire script. One of the scripts that Cohn sent her stood out from all the rest. It was a role that was unlike any other she had played before.

10
Winning It All

In July 1981, Marble Arch Productions announced that it had pur-
chased the film rights to William Styron's novel *Sophie's Choice* for
$750,000. Alan Pakula was hired to direct the picture. Rumors were
already circulating that it would be the most important film of the year.

As Meryl, Don and Henry were preparing to leave for England in May
1980, Cohn called Meryl to say that he had suggested her for the leading
role of Sophie Zowistowska. But Meryl was committed to *The French
Lieutenant's Woman*, and the script for *Sophie's Choice* was only partially
completed at that time. She opted to await her return from England before
giving Cohn a definite answer.

After returning to the United States, and finishing filming on *Stab!*,
Meryl was looking for a serious, important film. Cohn pirated a copy of the
now-completed script and sent it to Meryl. She immediately sensed the
power and challenge of the role and was ready to commit herself to it.

Pakula had postponed any decision on whom to cast as Sophie, choos-
ing first to sign an actor to play Nathan, Sophie's Jewish-intellectual lover.
Al Pacino lacked the correct touch of "bourgeois Jewishness." Dustin
Hoffman did not have Nathan's sadomasochistic romantic quality. Robert
De Niro had the necessary charisma, but not Nathan's humor. Unable to
make a decision, Pakula would continue to consider these three actors for
two years while he completed the script.

In the meantime, Pakula was deluged with actresses who wanted to
play Sophie. For a while, he seriously considered German-born actress
Marthe Keller, but passed her over in favor of his own personal choice,
Swedish actress Liv Ullmann. "She was 10 years older than Sophie," he told
the press, "but she could play the harsh realities and the ambivalences and
she was a woman with whom a young boy would fall in love."[1] He particularly liked Ullmann's "alien European quality"[2] that he considered crucial
to Sophie's personality.

If production had begun in 1979, Ullmann would have had the part.
But Pakula insisted on writing the script himself, which delayed production for another two years. He interrupted his writing to direct *Rollover*
with Jane Fonda and Kris Kristofferson. Ullmann, who had other film commitments, declined the role of Sophie.

While Pakula completed the script, Polish director Andrzej Wajda suggested Meryl. At the same time, one of Pakula's assistants in Europe telephoned to say he had found an exciting unknown actress there named Magda Vasaryova. Eventually, Pakula narrowed his choice to these two actresses for Sophie.

As he was deliberating which actress would win the role, Pakula attended a performance of *The Pirates of Penzance* and was impressed with Kevin Kline as the pirate king. "I was dazzled," he told a reporter. "He had a certain capacity for joy, the life force, the humor so essential for Nathan."[3] He immediately asked Kline to read for the part; as he had expected, Kline was perfect for the role, and Pakula signed him on the spot.

Now that the part of Nathan had been filled, it became decision time for the role of Sophie. In mid–July, Sam Cohn contacted Pakula, stating that Meryl had decided that she would commit herself to the part if it were still available. Pakula told Cohn that he would make his decision within the next ten days. Meryl followed up Cohn's call with one of her own, and Pakula repeated his promise of a decision in a few days. "O.K.," said Meryl, "but whether I play the role or not, I'll tell you who would make a wonderful Nathan — Kevin Kline."[4] Meryl had seen Kline in *Pirates* before going to England; so enthralled was she with his performance that she rushed backstage to tell him, "I'll appear with you in anything."[5]

Kline had begun his acting career under John Houseman, appearing in a number of productions of the prestigious Acting Company. He then appeared in *On the Twentieth Century*, for which he won a Tony Award. (He would eventually win another Tony as the pirate king in *The Pirates of Penzance*). When Pakula telephoned Meryl that she had the role of Sophie, Meryl was ecstatic, both for the part and the opportunity to appear opposite Kline.

When Peter MacNicol was signed to play the role of "Stingo," the naive young writer who is witness to the love affair of Sophie and Nathan, the major characters had all been signed. Now the $12 million project was ready to enter production.

Sophie's Choice is the heart-rending story of a woman who has survived the horror or a Nazi death camp, and comes to the United States immediately after World War II. The story is told through Stingo, a young man who has come to New York to become a writer. He takes a room at "The Pink Palace," a boarding house in Brooklyn. As he is moving in, he witnesses a blood-chilling argument between Sophie Zowistowska, a beautiful blonde Polish woman, and her Jewish lover, Nathan Landau, who walks out on her. Later that night, Sophie brings a snack down to Stingo and clumsily apologizes for the public argument. Stingo is entranced by Sophie, charmed by her malapropisms (she offers him a drink, calling it a "nighthat"). Nathan returns after midnight and the two lovers become reunited in a torrid love scene.

Sophie (Streep) and Nathan (Kevin Kline) pop into Stingo's window to invite him out in this scene from Sophie's Choice.

The next morning, Stingo is awakened by Sophie and a contrite Nathan dressed in bizarre period costumes. Accepting their invitation to accompany them to Coney Island, Stingo quickly develops a close friendship with the two lovers. The summer is passed between his trying to finish his novel and serving as adoring witness to their love affair.

But Stingo soon learns that both Sophie and Nathan have dark secrets. Nathan alternates between moments of endearing charm and maniacal rages laced with threats of violence. Stingo later discovers from Nathan's brother that he is a schizophrenic imposter, rather than the medical researcher that he claims to be.

Sophie's secret forms the central plot of the film. Gradually, Stingo catches her in repeated lies about her father, her life and her internment in a concentration camp. Finally, in a long, dispirited monologue, she reveals to Stingo her secret: An S.S. officer in the camp had forced her to choose which of her children would die in the gas chamber. Sophie had sacrificed her daughter to save her son; later her son died in the camp as well. Her subsequent life had been spent trying to escape reality and learning to cope with her guilt.

Stingo urges Sophie to leave Nathan and return with him to his Virginia home. They have one night of love at a motel. When Stingo awakes, he finds a note from Sophie telling him that she must stay with Nathan. Returning to the Brooklyn boardinghouse, Stingo finds Sophie and Nathan lying in bed, victims of a suicide pact. He returns to Virginia a chastened but infinitely wiser man.

Meryl was delighted in Pakula's approach to directing. Jane Fonda, upon hearing that Meryl had won the part, called her, saying, "You have no idea what's in store for you, working with Alan Pakula."[6] Meryl discovered what Fonda meant when she appeared on the set the first day. Unlike other film directors, Pakula insisted on an almost fanatical attention to reality. To achieve this, he had three weeks of rehearsals before filming began. He had the actual actors read their offscreen cues during close-ups of other members of the cast, rather than an anonymous prompter. He also forsook building a set for the concentration camp scenes in the United States; instead, he stated his intention to take the entire cast and crew to Yugoslavia to build a set there. By this means, he could recreate the feeling of the camps near their actual locations in Europe.

For the role of Sophie, Meryl's talent for mimicry and foreign accents came into full play, even more than in *The French Lieutenant's Woman*. She spent five days a week for three months studying Polish, then practicing her Polish accent in English to get the correct inflection. This rigorous regimen paid off. Styron, who served as technical consultant on the film, was impressed with her artistic exactitude. "Meryl's performance is simply the most amazing that I've ever seen," he later told the press. "I've known many Polish women, and I was astounded by her flawless accent."[7] Indeed, her acquisition of the accent was so thorough that she could not get rid of it. She was surprised once when she came home and leaned over Henry's crib and spoke to him; recognizing the face but not the voice, he burst out crying.

Then Meryl began the meticulous dissection of the character of Sophie. After much intense rereading of Styron's novel and much introspection, she could see Sophie clearly. She was "a great character with a lot of corners. Very sexy and funny, sometimes pathetic. Definitely not one of your noble people."[8]

Having conceived of Sophie's personality, Meryl set about creating the visual character. Launching herself on a strict diet, she reduced her fluid intake to lose ten pounds for the concentration camp scenes. Special makeup helped to achieve the emaciated look.

Of all her roles, Meryl was most excited about Sophie, understanding her far better than Joanna Kramer or Sarah Woodruff. "At first I had no idea what I was going to do with Sophie. It was only after I learned Polish and found Sophie's mouth beginning to make sounds in a certain way that I began to really know her."[9]

Kevin Kline was somewhat nervous about making the transition from the stage to film, and later acknowledged his great debt to Meryl for helping make the adjustment. Not that he needed any help in delineating Nathan's character; he saw Nathan as clearly as Meryl saw Sophie, perhaps more so. "Nathan is a fascinating character," he said during an interview. "His passion, his heroic qualities—he was born in the wrong century, he was trying to live a heroic life in an unheroic age. He was completely deluded, of course. But I adore his sense of humor, as vicious and as harmful as it was, it was also joyous! This man was capable of a tremendous appreciation of life. He loved life, and he hated it. He could listen to Beethoven and be absolutely filled with his love for the music, and yet he toys with death, flirts with death, even as he is living much more intensely than we are. He has a wonderful sense of ritual, a sense of event. And his sense of truth: he's living a lie, and yet he sees truth as only a mad person can. He lived with the horror of life; the rest of us are protected by our so-called sanity."[10]

Meryl refused to allow the film to interfere with her roles as wife and mother. After filming each day, she went home to fix supper and spend time with Don and Henry. This hectic pace took its toll on Meryl physically, but it won her the admiration and respect of her director. Pakula told the press during filming: "As a man, I don't know how that's done. . . . But I do know that it gave Meryl a sense of reality and stability all through shooting. Many lesser talents with whom I've worked are more precious about their gifts."[11]

Pakula, realizing what a unique artist Meryl was, made no attempt to overdirect Meryl. "I would never push Meryl into any direction of my own until I saw the direction she chose to take. Often, it was not what mine would have been; but it had more authenticity, more originality. The biggest thing you can do for an actress as gifted as Meryl Streep is to have the reality there for her to react to."[12]

Meryl responded enthusiastically to the hands-off approach that Pakula took to his stars, allowing them artistic freedom to develop their characters as they saw them. "As an actress," she said recently, "sometimes you edit yourself, because you don't have—faith. You don't have faith that your bad stuff will be gotten rid of, so you sort of direct yourself. I do it—a lot. And it's not a great thing, because you sometimes hold in check things that might develop into something interesting. You don't know where it will lead, especially in emotional scenes, so you kind of hold back. With Alan, I feel totally safe and . . . unedited."[13]

The only difficulty between Meryl and Pakula arose over his promise to her to build an Auschwitz set in Eastern Europe. Three weeks before the crew was scheduled to fly to Yugoslavia, Marble Arch balked at the expense of the trip. Meryl considered it essential to bringing Sophie to life on the screen to actually be on the site of all the horrors that took place in her life. It would not achieve the same effect just to make a replica in the United States, or—worse yet— to have Sophie merely *tell* Stingo about the experience. "Suddenly I got paranoid," she recalls, "that they weren't going to shoot that part in Europe at all—that they'd just let Sophie tell the story."[14] She angrily telephoned Pakula, accusing him of reneging on his promise, assuring him that it would ruin the authenticity of the film. Pakula renewed his promise, effectively arguing to the board of Marble Arch Productions how important the sequence was to the success of the film. In fact, he did more than that; he arranged for Kitty Hart, an Auschwitz survivor, to be present and tell Meryl in detail what it was like to be a woman in the camp.

Once in Yugoslavia, Meryl had second thoughts about her insistence on the location. This time, Don could not go with her because he had a one-man show opening in New York, and Meryl thought it best not to disrupt Henry's routine by taking him with her. After several weeks, the separation was too much for her. "The first week I was away, I felt great. The second week, I went into a stupor. And the third week, I sort of went crazy because I missed Don and Henry so much."[15]

In addition to missing her family, Meryl felt guilty at not being in New York for the opening of Don's show; after all, he had always been present for the premieres of her films. She wrote a note to Pakula, asking him if she could fly home on Saturday, attend the gallery opening on Sunday and fly back to Yugoslavia for work on Monday. "Don's always there for me," she wrote. "Now I'm eating myself up that I can't be there for him."[16]

It was a quandary for Pakula; on the one hand, he understood her loneliness and guilt, but on the other, he had the responsibility of the entire production to consider. Did she have the strength to fly all that way, suffer jet lag, attend the function and return for work the next day? He could not shoot around her and could not hold up production while his star recovered. There was always the chance that she would miss the connecting flights and production would be at a standstill for several days.

But Pakula had faith in Meryl. "I trusted her totally," he would recall later. "And I knew that not being there *would* eat her up." Few directors would have allowed it, but he agreed, even putting her on the flight himself. Meryl endured two grueling transatlantic flights, was a charming wife by Don's side and returned to the set. Pakula was astounded by her tenacity and endurance. "She was back on Monday . . . and her work was terrific."[17]

Critical reception of *Sophie's Choice* was mixed. The critics thought the extended flashback when Sophie reveals her past to Stingo was disruptive to the film's progression. Nor was the rationale for Sophie or Nathan's persona entirely convincing. But the critics were in unanimous agreement about the high quality of the acting.

Janet Maslin of the *New York Times* noted: "The heroine of William

Styron's 'Sophie's Choice' is a creature of such extravagant and contradictory attributes that the role would be difficult for any actress, even by an actress of extraordinary resourcefulness and versatility. Meryl Streep has already established herself as a performer of that calibre. Miss Streep accomplishes the near-impossible, presenting Sophie in believable human terms without losing the scale of Mr. Styron's invention. In a role affording every opportunity for overstatement, she offers a performance of such measured intensity that the results are by turns exhilarating and heartbreaking. Thanks in large part to Miss Streep's bravura performance, it's a film that casts a powerful, uninterrupted spell." Ms. Maslin was particularly impressed with the extended monologue in which Sophie confesses her lies to Stingo. "The character's halting, Polish-accented speech, her charming malapropisms, her frank sexuality (something Miss Streep conveys easily without any need for nudity), her long, haunted reminiscences — these are the components of an unforgettable heroine and the work of the astonishing actress who brings her to life."

Richard Corliss of *Time*, however, was put off by the thirty-minute flashback in the middle of the film, believing that it could best be done in a short narration. But he considered the acting of the cast as nothing short of superb. "Kevin Kline is an engaging actor who can play both ends of passion, the delightful and the deranged." Corliss was especially enthusiastic about Meryl. "Miss Streep's performance is a seamless, seductive piece. Sophie's past justifies Streep's familiar mannerisms: the wistful, knowing smile, the nervous fingers burrowing into a copse of hair, the starts and stops of dialogue, even the red blotches on her skin during moments of high tension. Here it is one more challenge that this galvanizing actress sets for herself, a total immersion in character, a necessary step toward revelation. As Sophie, Streep is fine and beautiful and a little heartbreaking."

David Denby of *New York* magazine added: "Meryl Streep is perhaps the first actress since the young Ingrid Bergman to make desolation ravishingly sexy." But Denby was not as enthusiastic about the film itself. "Streep is great, but she's virtually the whole movie." He credited Kline's performance, but regarded him as "still a theatrical actor," and dismissed MacNicol's role as "unperformable." Denby's primary criticism was that Sophie's monologue to Stingo was much too long, as were Nathan's rantings, and that the flashback failed in its purpose of revealing Sophie's character. "This is an undramatic, morally simple movie, a movie about the Holocaust so softly lyrical that it could almost be called genteel."

Pauline Kael considered *Sophie's Choice* to be an "infuriatingly bad movie . . . stuffed with literary references and encrusted with the weighty culture of big themes: evil, tortured souls, guilt." Primarily, the flaws in the film, as Kael saw it, were a result of Pakula's almost slavish adherence to the novel, and Styron's lugubrious prose. "The movie is a novel being talked to us. And Styron's novel is all come-on." Kael thought that even the momentous climax to which the film was building fell flat. "The whole plot is based on a connection that isn't there," she wrote, "the connection between Sophie and Nathan's relationship (Catholic and Jew), and what the Nazis did to the Jews." The whole plot was predicated upon the revelation of Sophie's terrible choice, but Kael felt that it did not produce the intended effect. "The incident is garish rather than illuminating, and too particular to demonstrate anything general. The inert movie takes the book so seriously that you may feel it's Pakula who is the sucker."

Nor was Kael any kinder to the cast. "As Sophie, Meryl Streep is colorful in the first, campy, late-forties scenes . . . red-lipped with bright-golden curls, she dimples flirtatiously and rattles on in Polish-accented, broken English, making her seem zany." Even the comic scenes where Sophie makes atrocious malapropisms, which many critics found endearing, failed to impress Kael. "I felt more sympathy for Meryl Streep the actress trying to put over these scenes, than I could for Sophie herself." As in her reviews of Meryl's previous films, Kael was willing to praise Meryl for being an accomplished technician. "Streep is very beautiful at times, and she does amusing, nervous bits of business, like fidgeting with a furry boa—her fingers twiddling with our heartstrings. She has, as usual, put thought and effort into her work." To Kael, Sophie was merely a pawn in an ethnic guilt-and-evil game between Portestant, Catholic and Jew, with little character or personality to be developed, even by as talented an actress as Meryl.

Kline and MacNicols came in for their share of Kael's invective as well. She considered MacNicols' role the only sustained performance in the film, but even his was a "lifeless part," as on-looker to the sadomasochism of Nathan and Sophie. Nor did she have any praise for Kevin Kline. "Kline is saddled with the kind of flamboyant role that never works—the suffering genius. It's an unplayable part—there's not a single believable moment in it."

Stanley Kauffmann was offended by the triteness of the film clichés, as when Stingo balances on his shoulders a tottering case of Spam, which, predictably, topples. Or when the camera focuses in for a close-up of the shaking chandelier to indicate the torrid sex scene going on in Nathan and Sophie's room above Stingo. Like Kael, Kauffmann thought the film suffered from too closely following Styron's "grandiose prose" and "gummy rhetoric." Primarily, however, the principal flaw was the same as he found in the book: The story had no center and no protagonist. The action surrounding Sophie's choice is so far into the past that it can be recalled only in a tedious flashback. To Kauffmann, Nathan is not so much a character as a pathological caricature, evoking only a vague sympathy from the audience. MacNicols had nothing to do but watch the unfolding of Nathan and Sophie's doomed love affair, "merely occupying space without dramatic justification."

But Kauffmann had no reservations concerning Meryl Streep. "Her performance of Sophie is the film's sole achievement," he observed. "She looks more translucently beautiful than ever, and she has the Polish accent right. What Streep has wrought . . . is a psychological verity for Sophie that she reveals through patterns of motion . . . shunning the scrutiny of others. . . . The overall impression of her movement is sidling, gently attempting to hide herself in open space. Through this kinetic concept, Streep gives Sophie an aura of concealment. . . . She is not revealing her whole self to anyone. Sometimes Pakula hands the picture over to Streep. She handles these moments like a virtuoso."

Kauffmann was particularly fond of two scenes in the film. One was when Sophie is telling Stingo about her father in a lyrical, whimsical tone while playing with a feather boa. "She plays off the boa adroitly, but cleverly." At that time, she deliberately plays with the word "Christ," telling Stingo that she felt it was a time when Christ turned away from her. "The tiny pause just before it, the slow formation of the first consonants, the suspension of the middle, the almost reluctant close of the word. She makes the monosyllable an utterance. It's wonderful. Very, very few American actors could do it. The value of the film is Streep's richness." As for the two other principal characters, he dismissed them in short order. Kline "works feverishly. He has great energy and fire, but can't fuse fragments of a demented character into a schizoid whole . . . a series of ecstatic and furious bits." MacNicols is a "pleasant youth."

Surprisingly, when the Academy Award nominations were announced in February 1983, *Sophie's Choice* was not among the final five nominees, but it was pitted against formidable competition in a strong field: *Das Boot*, *The Verdict*, *Tootsie*, *Gandhi* and *E.T.*

But no one was surprised that Meryl was nominated for her heartrending portrayal of Sophie. Her competition in the Best Actress category was outstanding as well. Julie Andrews was nominated as the male impersonator in *Victor/Victoria*, Sissy Spacek for her role as the wife of an American murdered in Chile in *Missing*, Debra Winger as a factory worker desperate to marry a naval air cadet in *An Officer and a Gentleman* and Jessica Lange for her role as a fiery actress placed in a mental institution in *Frances*. Lange was Meryl's closest competition, with her evocative performance as the free-spirited, self-destructive Frances Farmer. The two roles of Sophie and Frances were very similar; both were, as one commentator put it, "divine masochists, and Hollywood loves divine masochists."[18] Hollywood also loves tradition. Lange was nominated for Best Supporting Actress as well, for her part as the radiantly soft sex object in *Tootsie*; no one since Teresa Wright in 1942 had been nominated for both categories in the same year, and speculation was rife that she might be the first actress to win both awards.

On April 11, *Ghandi* walked away with most of the major awards — Best Picture, Best Actor (Ben Kingsley), Best Director and Best Screenplay, despite a growing prejudice against British films and the fact that *Chariots of Fire* had won the previous year. Jessica Lange did receive Best Supporting Actress for *Tootsie*, but Meryl finally was awarded the coveted Best Actress Oscar, an event that many felt was long overdue. Unlike the ceremony in 1979, Meryl was more composed and gave a long recitation of "thank you's" that included not only the expected kudos to her co-stars, director and producer, but virtually every member of the crew as well. At long last she was undeniably "bankable." More importantly, she had achieved that most elusive of all Hollywood categories: superstar.

If her personal life had been difficult after winning the Oscar in 1980, it became even more so once she was proclaimed Best Actress. "Privacy is very hard to come by these days," she explained. "I don't like being self-conscious twenty-four hours a day. You think it was easy for me when *Life* magazine proclaimed me 'America's Best Actress'? My friends wouldn't speak to me for weeks. Excessive hype like that is very destructive. There is no such thing as 'best' in my field, and proclaiming otherwise makes newspaper wraps for tomorrow's fish."[19]

In addition to *Life* magazine, she also appeared on the cover of *Newsweek, Time, Rolling Stone,* the *New York Times Magazine* and dozens of other publications. "Nobody believes that stuff!" she continued. "Just sit around the actors' bars and listen to what they're saying. 'What *is* this about Meryl Streep? I don't think she's so great.' People need superlatives. But the quality of my work, as of anybody's, varies with the project."[20]

Her sense of values remained intact after the Oscar and media hype. When asked by reporters what the first thing was that she did after receiving the Oscar, she confided to a rush of extravagance: She and Don went out and bought a washer, dryer and a Cuisinart, all of which she said were handy to have with a baby in the house. To escape the pressure from interviews and photograph sessions, she, Don and Henry retreated more and more frequently to their tree farm in Duchess County. Her few public appearances were to participate in a rally at Central Park for the Equal Rights Amendment, narrate a film on nuclear disarmament and give a speech on sexism in films. Her most fervent commitment was to nuclear disarmament. On the rare occasions when she would speak on the subject during interviews, she made a passionate appeal for public awareness and involvement. "We've got to write letters to our congressmen. We can't withdraw into a deadening, frightened end-of-the-world fear, so deeply rooted that we don't even recognize it in ourselves. I keep thinking all the time that in the year 2000 Henry will be only twenty-one."[21]

Other than occasional interviews and public appearances, Meryl remained a homebody for several months, trying to re-establish contact with her family and friends. "When I work I put in fifteen-hour days and I can manage to keep up only with Don and Henry and perhaps two or three other people. My greatest regret is that I don't have fuller relationships with my friends. My idea of a good friend is my mother, who drops everything if a friend is sick or in trouble. But then, she's never on location in Austria."[22]

Both Meryl and Don were determined to keep their home lives simple and not succumb to the temptations of "going Hollywood." They were noticeably absent from the trendy party scene in New York, limiting their outings to occasional visits to the theater and their favorite restaurants.

Meryl began to come to terms with combining her career and home life. The most difficult was leaving little Henry. "But when I am home for months on end, ten hours a day," she said, "my son gets sick of me. When I'm away, he's fine. It becomes routine that I'm not around. It's when we keep switching the rhythm that it becomes confusing to him. . . . He can handle it, he's always been very centered—not a race-around-tear-'em-up kind of kid."[23]

If the Oscar is the most coveted honor for an actor or actress, those within the profession also know that it often carries with it a curse, that is, the next film of the winner is often a box-office bomb. This gloomy prediction held true for Meryl when *Stab!* was released in December 1982, shortly after *Sophie's Choice.*

Benton finally released the film under the new title *Still of the Night.* The critics universally panned it—and for the first time in her career, not even Meryl's performance escaped the scathing reviews.

Michael Sragow of *Rolling Stone* dubbed it a "stultifying thriller whose central murder mystery has been refined out of existence." Because of the Upper East Side setting of the film, it was constantly being compared with *Kramer vs. Kramer,* but this time the critics did not find the situation remotely believable, with no rationale for Scheider and Meryl to fall in love. The suspense was dull and flat, with obvious red herrings that do not prevent the audience from guessing who the killer is halfway through the film. Most criticized was the contrived ending which placed Brooke, Sam and the killer together at the climax. The principal weakness was the hokey renditions of Hitchcock classics, most notably *North by Northwest* and *Vertigo;* if Benton had intended it to be a tribute to Hitchcock, he failed miserably in the eyes of the critics, who thought he was merely ripping off the master. Instead of suspenseful, the critics saw it as "melodramatically intense."

Previously, when critics had been ambivalent about one of Meryl's films, they had at least credited her performance, often considering her portrayal of the heroine to have either saved the film or at least been its sole redeeming grace. This time, however, Meryl shared the abysmal fate of the film, perhaps because she was not given any scenes to develop Brooke's personality beyond the superficial one of a strikingly beautiful and hapless neurotic. As the *Rolling Stone* critic put it, "Streep is far too brittle to convey the allure intended, yet probably no one could breathe life into such a cartoon figure.... Whenever Streep plays a disconnected character, she loses any emotional depth. When she plays a rooted character—as in *The Deadliest Season* or *The Deer Hunter*—she can have a rough-hewed elegance. But as the cultural heiress, she's . . . all fuss and flutter."

Pauline Kael was particularly offended at both the transparent borrowing of style and theme from Hitchcock and the ineffectual way in which Benton tried to present it. "'Still of the Night' is reticent and soft where it should be tough.... The film shows almost no evidence of the nasty streak that's part of the pleasure of a good thriller, or the manipulative skills that might give us a few tremors. Was the plot so clear in Benton's mind that he trimmed away the explanations, thinking we would be able to figure it all out? As a director Benton seems unable to find any rhythm in the scenes.... We don't feel the tug of the doctor being drawn to the inscrutable blonde, and we never shudder for the danger he's in. The most dramatic thing about the movie happens offscreen: Meryl Streep switches the part in her hair from one side to the other."

Kael also saw Meryl's talent as completely wasted in the film, reduced to a "Veronica Lake kittenish act, but without her teasing, kitty-cat charm." What Kael saw as missing in Meryl's portrayal of Brooke were the subtle nuances that had made Joanna Kramer and Sarah Woodruff such memorable and sympathetic characters. "In most of the rest of this movie, she doesn't resemble a living person; her face is gaunt, her skin has become alabaster. She seems to have chosen to do a Meryl Streep parody. Streep has been falling into the trap of selecting noble roles—the martyrs, the drippers. And she makes this femme fatale seem more zombified than anything else. I liked Streep on the stage, but I have come to dread her reflective manner and flooding tears—she could give pensive a bad name. If only she would giggle more and suffer less—she keeps turning herself into the red-eye special."

Roy Scheider fared no better in Kael's estimation. "Why is Roy Scheider so dull? He isn't an incompetent actor, and he's actually rather accomplished here—he's at least restrained. But he has no visible personality."

Newsweek's David Ansen also clucked his tongue at the inability of Benton to more effectively utilize the extraordinary talents of his co-stars, and was puzzled at why Benton felt compelled to resurrect such a dated plot, especially when Hitchcock had so thoroughly put his stamp on its plot devices. "One can only mourn the waste of talent and wonder what possessed Benton to drag out this tired old script. A thriller in which a psychiatrist solves the murder by interpreting a dream? There hasn't been such a dime-store Freudian gimmick since the days when there were dime stores. Flirting with Hitchcock's ghost is a dangerous game. Benton's movie is coldly academic; he doesn't add anything to his Hitchcockian

In this scene from Still of the Night, *Dr. Sam Rice (Roy Scheider) opens a gift from Brooke Reynolds (Streep): a small figurine to replace one she broke in his office.*

aspirations and he hasn't concocted a story strong enough to stand on its own." The similarities between classic Hitchcockian roles so memorably created by Cary Grant and Grace Kelly caused Ansen to view the performances of Meryl and Scheider unfavorably by comparison. "Scheider and Streep are no Grant and Kelly; you can't strike a flame with two metallic matches. Streep's taut neuroticism never yields to eroticism, and there's not a relaxed muscle in Scheider's body."

Richard Schickel of *Time* faulted the film primarily for Benton's preoccupation with trying to create a slick style rather than a multi-leveled plot, and the film's own self-importance over creation of characters with any depth. "*Still of the Night* is an irritating and unsatisfying film. For a movie about a series of gory knife murders . . . it has an oddly reverential hush about it. This seems to arise less from a regard for the Hitchcock tradition than from a quiet appreciation of its own classiness. Lacking the old boy's schizophrenic sensibility, Benton can do no more than offer a dispassionate mimicry of someone else's style." Like Ansen, Schickel was disappointed in Benton's attempt to make the characterizations of Rice and Brooke into ersatz Cary Grant and Grace Kelly performances. "Scheider is sober, stalwart and workmanlike, but one longs for the goofy exasperation Cary Grant used to bring to roles like this. . . . Streep fares better. She is either the homicidal maniac the police suspect she is, or a woman driven to paranoid frenzy by those suspicions. Either way, she is an actress with a proven ability to suggest neurotic fires burning beneath a cool surface and the knack for enlisting a sympathy we know may be misplaced."

Schickel may have been kinder to Meryl than he was to Scheider—if ever so faintly—but it remained for Meryl's long-time admirer in the *New York Times*, Vincent Canby, to give the sole favorable review of the film and her performance in it: "'Still of the Night' is an intelligently entertaining movie with two quite striking weaknesses. The resolution to the mystery, although logical, isn't either strong or eccentric enough to support the emotional desperation that precedes it. The second—and much greater—problem is the total lack of electricity between the ravishingly beautiful, possibly lost lady played by Miss Streep and the previously commonsensical doctor, who jeopardizes his career and his life to help her against the better instincts of everyone else.

"I'm not sure whether this is a result of the casting or the writing and the directing. Mr. Scheider, an excellent actor, is too intense—too serious, really—to suggest the wildly unexpected romantic nature that the doctor discovers in himself, after his first meeting with the woman who before had only been his mind's dark vision. Miss Streep is stunning, but she's not on screen anywhere near long enough."

Fortunately for Meryl, her next film would erase the unhappy memory of *Still of the Night*, and restore her to public and critical acclaim. Before that, Meryl was recognized by the academic world by addressing the one hundred and nineteenth commencement of her alma mater, Vassar, and receiving an honorary Doctor of Fine Arts from the Graduate School and University Center of the City University of New York.

In her remarks to the graduating class, Meryl told the graduates that they should "engage in an attempt for excellence"[24] just as Vassar had instilled in her a "taste for excellence."[25] Continuing this theme to the more than 4000 graduates, parents, alumni and faculty, Meryl said: "Demand the best of your leaders. Take your heart to work. Ask the best of yourself and everyone else, too." She cautioned the graduates that they may face severe challenges and setbacks. "But you must look your dilemmas in the face and decide what is best for you. If you can live with the devil, then Vassar has not sunk its teeth into you."[26] At the conclusion of her remarks, the audience gave Meryl a standing ovation.

In conferring upon Meryl the honorary Doctor of Fine Arts, Dr. Harold M. Proshansky, president of the Graduate School and University Center of the City University of New York, told the assembled graduates and dignitaries that Meryl was being given the degree for being "one of the most intelligent, perceptive and sensitive young American actresses."[27]

These two honors were particularly satisfying to Meryl after the critical drubbing she had received after *Still of the Night* was released. In her next film, she would prove to the critics that the words that she used to inspire the Vassar class of 1983, and the praise that she had received at City University, were both accurate in terms of her commitment to her craft and in describing her talent.

11
Silkwood

Silkwood was something of a phenomenon in contemporary American film—an artistic film with a strong political message reminiscent of the "social consciousness" films of the 1930s. Yet director Mike Nichols and screenwriters Nora Ephron and Alice Arlen kept the polemics to a minimum while telling a human story of unexceptional blue collar characters caught in the sweep of extraordinary events and dangers.

The central character of the film is the late Karen Silkwood (Meryl Streep), a flippant, hip-swinging, profane maverick who works as a lab analyst at the Kerr-McGee plutonium plant near Cimarron, Oklahoma. Karen lives with her boyfriend, Drew (Kurt Russell), and Dolly (Cher Bono Allman). She is unconcerned about the possible dangers of her job until she is contaminated. When Karen begins to investigate rumors of deliberate falsification of photographs of faulty fuel rods for nuclear reactors, she comes to believe that she is being harassed by Kerr-McGee; perhaps her own contamination is an attempt to frighten her into abandoning what quickly becomes an obsession to collect evidence to expose the company's willful negligence.

In her zealous pursuit of evidence, Karen becomes active in the Oil, Chemical and Atomic Workers Union, which is headed by diffident lackeys who are ineffectual in fighting an attempt by Kerr-McGee to get the union decertified. Because her activities threaten the closing of the plant, Karen is ostracized by her co-workers. The tension even causes a break with Drew, who cannot take the pressure applied to him by the company and his own co-workers. Karen is eventually fired, but not before she, Drew and Dolly are tested; but only Karen is found to be internally contaminated, a virtual death sentence. There is the possibility that Dolly, under intimidation from the company, informed them of Karen's clandestine investigation, and that Karen's contamination may have been deliberate on the part of Kerr-McGee or one of her colleagues.

As Karen becomes increasingly ill, she turns in desperation to an official in the national union headquarters in New York (Paul Stone), with whom she has a brief affair. It soon becomes apparent that he is not particularly concerned about Karen's individual fate; he sees the issue only as an effective weapon against Kerr-McGee's attempt to decertify the union. When Karen desperately needs his advice on combatting company pressures on her, she is unable to reach him, having to tearfully convey her fears to his answering machine. Karen is a pathetic figure, a loner fighting a hopeless battle against a huge corporation without the cooperation of her co-workers, unaided by uncaring union officials, abandoned by her lover and possibly betrayed by her closest friend.

Her only assistance from the national union is to be put in contact with a *New York Times* reporter. Karen arranges a meeting with the reporter at a motel outside of Cimarron to show him the evidence she has compiled against the company. On her way to the meeting, her car is gradually over-taken by intimidating headlights. Moments later, Karen is killed in a one-car accident. The film ends with the solemn voice of Karen singing "Amazing Grace."

From such unsettling source material, Nichols and the cast produced a troubling, sensitive film. Here Meryl had a very different type of role from anything she had previously done. Her previous screen roles had been sophisticated women; Karen was the antithesis of urbanity. She was earthy, profane and sexually promiscuous in the film. Silkwood had been a woman who defied the stereotypical role of wife and mother, leaving her children in the custody of her common-law husband to work as a lab technician for Kerr-McGee. But, unlike Joanna Kramer, she did not leave to "find herself." Nor did she suffer societal ostracism to live the life of a recluse like Sarah Woodruff. On the contrary, she was a feisty, intelligent, politically sophisticated union activist who pitted herself against a corporate conglomerate in a one-sided battle that ultimately led to her death.

It was widely rumored that Meryl took the role because of her activism against nuclear disarmament and the dangers of nuclear energy, but Meryl denied that was her motivation. "I accepted the part not because it meshes with my feelings about nuclear disarmament," she said in an interview on the set, "but because it has a very good script—which is rare."[1] She also saw in Karen Silkwood a much more complex individual than was presented in the mythology that surrounded her shortly after her death. "I was attracted to the character," she continued. "What I liked about Karen was that she wasn't Joan of Arc at all. She was unsavory in some ways and yet she did some very good things. I have to be presented with a certain challenge and a character with problems. This doesn't feel like an anti-nuclear movie. There are lots of those around, and I've stayed away from them quite purposefully because I don't like polemics. It has the feeling of real working life, and I think it's about that more than anything nuclear."[2]

Meryl would have to mold a complicated character to encompass the contradictory nature of the real Karen Silkwood. Unlike Kurt Russell, who lived with the real-life Drew Stephens in order to learn more about him,

Meryl had to mold the personality of Karen Silkwood from what she had read about her and her own visceral instincts of what a woman from Karen's background would do and how she would act in such a situation. "I was meeting no one; all I had were pieces of information from different sources. I had details from five or six people that all described a different woman."[3]

Besides her rural roots and eccentric lifestyle, the role would have to thread a difficult course to show the many sides of her personality. "She wasn't settled," Meryl said in assessing Karen. "She was always looking for trouble. There are people who are always exploring possibilities, looking around to make waves. That was the way she seemed to me. She was a very difficult person. My heart breaks for her. She was only twenty-eight or twenty-nine when she died, and it was a real waste. I'm really glad I got the chance to try to step into her shoes for awhile."[4]

As the movie progresses, Meryl moves from one trait to another: stubbornness, moral laxity, contempt for authority and a basic "I-don't-give-a-damn" mentality. This could quickly have degenerated into a "good ol' gal" stereotype. But Meryl is able to blend in the other parts of Silkwood's character: intelligence, genuine sensitivity, and, finally, a gradually developed commitment to change things, even at the expense of corporate intimidation and ostracism from her co-workers, friends and lover.

For the role, Meryl cropped her hair, and — to end once and for all the image of the delicate, vulnerable woman that had been so much a part of her career to date — she swore, wisecracked and exuded sexual promiscuity by flashing a breast to a corporate official. Meryl plays Karen as a sassy, resolutely average woman caught up in extraordinary circumstances. As Silkwood, Meryl has a decidedly earthy look and manner. Karen Silkwood is sensuous, but not in the patrician manner of Sarah Woodruff, nor the remote manner of Sophie Zowistowska. But Meryl presents more subtle nuances to Karen's personality than just the sensual free spirit. She generates tremendous emotional power as Karen when she realizes that she has been exposed to radioactive materials. There are harrowing scenes of co-workers scrubbing her skin after she has been "cooked" from radiation exposure.

Once she is contaminated, an on-screen transformation occurs in Karen. The healthy, active Silkwood becomes more and more a tired, irritable woman whose body, if not her determination, is being ground down, hollowed out. Meryl had just completed the concentration camp scenes in Yugoslavia for *Sophie's Choice* three weeks before. To convey the sickly Karen Silkwood, Meryl again submitted to a rigorous diet, drinking a concoction from a blender in her trailer, and the skill of makeup expert Roy Helland completed the effect of Karen's physical deterioration.

"Silkwood was a thin girl to begin with," explained Meryl, "and as her troubles mounted, as she got more paranoid, she got thinner. I didn't kill myself to lose weight, though. I'd just finished the Auschwitz section on *Sophie's Choice*. Everybody says I look so harsh, but I loved it. In *Silkwood*, I think I look great."[5]

While on location in Texas, Meryl became friends with singer Cher Bono Allman. As Jane Fonda had taken Meryl under her wing on the set of *Julia*, so Meryl offered the same support to Cher in her first film role. She had seen Cher perform in the short-lived play *Come Back to the Five-and-Dime, Jimmy Dean, Jimmy Dean* earlier that year and admired her performance. "I was already in the mindset of 'my friend is coming. I have somebody on my side.'"[6]

To Cher, it was just the sort of reception she needed to offset her fear that she would be ridiculed on the set because of her reputation as an exhibitionist pop singer, rather than someone seriously trying to break into acting. "The first day on location," she recalls, "Meryl just came up, threw her arms around me and said, 'I'm so glad you're here.' She's all communication and warmth and friendship with a great sense of humor."[7]

During the three-and-a-half months of filming in Texas, their relationship quickly evolved into a deep, genuine friendship. Screenwriter Nora Ephron recalls, "It was my impression that Meryl made a very serious attempt to replicate their situation off-screen. They were together all the time. I can't overestimate how that friendship made it possible for Cher not to be wildly nervous."[8] On weekends, Meryl and Cher would take off driving to amusement parks with their children, Cher's Chastity and Elijah Blue, and Meryl's Henry, to malls, movies and rural barbecue joints, where they would do hilarious schticks, outlandish accents and fake fights before the amazed patrons. "They were hysterically funny together," remembers Ephron.[9]

But it was not all fun and games. Often the two would get together to have serious talks about their children or their private goals and ambitions in life. The talks were therapeutic for Cher, who was depressed that her children were unable to stay on the set as Henry stayed with Meryl. Meryl remembers how difficult those days were for Cher. "Cher would hole up in her room a lot. She can get very sad and go into black moods."[10]

But it took quite an adjustment for two such different personalities to mesh so well. Cher was flamboyant and liked to shock onlookers when they went on shopping sprees. Meryl remembers the first time they went out in public together soon after filming began. "I was appalled when we went to Six Flags once and Cher had this pink miniskirt on that was *maybe* six inches long in the back. And she just blithely walks through the place. I mean, I'd wear a wig and sunglasses and a trench coat. But Cher doesn't mind being the center of attention. It isn't agony for her. It doesn't take away part of her soul."[11]

Another striking difference between the two women was their attitude toward clothes. Cher recalls: "Meryl would make fun of the way I'd want to dress up every day. . . . And I'd say, 'Mary Louise, you've got to learn how to *dress.*'"[12] Whereas Cher would think nothing of spending a fortune on a single outing, Meryl would agonize over buying a single sweater, much to Cher's amusement. "Meryl couldn't care less what she wears. I'd tease her about that and she'd tell me to shut up. And she did her own ironing, which drove me insane. She says it keeps her down to earth."[13]

Despite the difference in their lifestyles, both Meryl and Cher found a great deal to admire in each other. Cher found Meryl to be a dedicated professional who taught her the discipline necessary to develop her latent dramatic talents, and also a close confidante and friend. "If she were my own sister," says Cher, "I couldn't love her more. People don't realize it, but Meryl's a funny, funny lady."[14] And Meryl, who constantly worried about the effect her career and fame would have on Henry, took a lesson from the relationship between Cher and her children. "Cher has a seven-year-old. When he really wants to torment her, he says, 'Are you *Cher?* Are you really *Cher?* Can I have your autograph, Cher?* She's at the top of her act now, maybe because she's not dependent on any man — she's brave with her ideas in a way women are often not. That's her savvy and smarts."[15]

There was an easy camaraderie between the crew, the cast and director Mike Nichols that made filming a pleasant, smooth-flowing process, which was fortunate, considering the pressures that were put on the film from outside sources. Given the nature of the film, Nichols found himself immersed in controversy from the beginning. Karen Silkwood's death aroused immediate media curiosity that still continues to this day. Antinuclear groups, unionists and feminists found in it a *cause célèbre*, and proponents of nuclear energy were quick to attack the allegations of wrongdoing by Kerr-McGee and suggestions that Silkwood was the victim of sinister machinations by the company or her co-workers. So much of the Silkwood case was shrouded in hearsay and innuendo that Nichols, Ephron and Arlen chose to concentrate upon the characters rather than the specific questions of whether Karen was deliberately contaminated, whether she really had solid evidence of malfeasance on the part of Kerr-McGee and what was the nature of the accident that took Karen's life on route to meet a newspaper reporter. These points were made ambiguous in the film; at the end there is a statement on film that no documents were found to incriminate the company and that traces of alcohol and barbiturates were found in Karen's bloodstream which could have caused her to fall asleep at the wheel. It was a difficult subject, one that could easily have led to a lawsuit by the company and by the individuals portrayed. The photomicrographs that Karen claimed were doctored to disguise defects in fuel rods were judged to be touch-ups of dust spots on the film; no

Streep in the title role of Silkwood.

evidence was found to indicate how Karen herself or her home was contaminated; and, although there were a number of documents found at the crash site of Karen's car, none revealed any duplicity by Kerr-McGee. Equally important, there was a suit against the company by Bill Silkwood, Karen's father, for $10 million in damages that was under appeal to the United States Supreme Court. Mr. Silkwood had originally made a claim against the company of $5000 for the destruction of Karen's home. When the company offered only $1500, he brought suit against them for $10 million, and won. But an appellate court threw out all but the original

$5000. Eventually, the Supreme Court reinstated the original decision against the company of $10 million. No one in the production company or the crew was anxious to see the film delayed because of litigation, but the final cut of the film clearly showed that Nichols' and Ephron's sympathies lay with the conspiracy theory.

Silkwood was released on December 19, 1983. Strong reaction was immediate, pro and con, over the subject matter. Kerr-McGee released a statement to the press that the film was "a highly fictionalized Hollywood dramatization scarcely connected to the facts." Karen's family and friends were quick to praise the film, but had reservations about the way the film characterized Karen. In trying to present a free-spirited individualist, Meryl and Nichols had emphasized Karen's maverick qualities: her deliberate vulgarity, sexually loose morals and her naivete about union practices in her one-sided fight against Kerr-McGee.

Sherri Ellis, Karen's real-life roommate (portrayed as Dolly Pelliker in the film) was outraged that the film suggested that she could have betrayed Karen to the company. "The upsetting thing is the insinuation that I could have snitched on Karen to the company," she told reporters. "But I sold the producers of the film the character-portrayal rights, and for $65,500 they can defame my character any way they want."[16]

Drew Stephens, who served as technical adviser to the film, resented the portrayal of Karen as an ignorant country girl, when in reality she was a straight–A student. He also disliked her being shown as dispirited in her battle with the company. "The last image I have of her," he said, "was the night we came back from Los Alamos. She was standing astride the heat register on the floor of my house with a Bloody Mary in her hand, and she said, 'We've got the mother------- now.' I'll never forget that, never."[17]

But it was Bill Silkwood who was the most offended of all. "The movie made her look not very bright and a hick *Tobacco Road* type," he says. "Karen was brilliant. I'll tell you what happened. The lawyers were scared of that damn movie, and [director] Mike Nichols didn't stick to his guns. Kerr-McGee portrayed her at the trial as a dopey, immoral person, and they kind of did that in the movie too."[18]

Regarding Karen's union activities and political awareness, Steve Wodka, the national union representative who met with Karen about her allegations against Kerr-McGee (and who was portrayed under a fictitious name in the film by Paul Stone) also disagreed with the depiction of Karen as naive. "She was a little more politically aware of what was going on than Streep portrays her. Karen had chutzpa, she had spunk. She cared a lot about her fellow workers."[19]

Film critics concentrated their reviews more on the presentation of the "evidence" of corporate culpability and conspiracy theories than on the quality of the film or the acting. *Time*'s Richard Schickel was offended at the "Joan of Arc" portrayal of Karen and the "martyred saint complex." He considered Karen Silkwood to be "demonstrably unstable . . . neurotically self-centered and very messy both in her private life and in her relationships with peers and superiors at work." Since there was no conscious commitment to a coherent program of opposition to the status quo in the film, there was no heroic stance by Silkwood based on a knowledge on her part of the risks that she was taking. To Schickel, the film was a "tissue of contradictory implications and politicized mythmaking" which failed to involve the audience at "a more intense and immediate dramatic emotional and intellectual level." Therefore, Karen's political acts and death had little meaning to the message inherent to the film. He also rejected the implication that the struggle against Kerr-McGee had somehow redeemed the inconsequential nature of her life. "The facts do not support a politically alarming or dramatically compelling conclusion.

Although Nichols' intention was to show blue-collar life, Schickel regarded that attempt a failure as well. He wrote that there was "none of the affectionate respect for working class life" that he found in *Norma Rae*, and "no instructive connection with Silkwood's milieu." Despite having highly praised Meryl's work in the past, Schickel thought she had seriously missed the mark in *Silkwood*. He noted that Meryl was "an actress of calculated effects, which works well when she is playing self-conscious intelligent women," but in *Silkwood* "she seems at once forced and pulled back." By contrast, he found Kurt Russell and Cher "sassier and more naturalistic performers."

Jack Kroll of *Newsweek* considered *Silkwood* "one of the best American films of the year. It makes you feel good about moviemaking." To Kroll, the film had style, energy and talent. It was a "powerful film, compelling entertainment in presenting fears of the nuclear age with its pains and problems. The virtue of *Silkwood* is that it brings such an issue down to real human lives, human flesh, human weaknesses and strengths." Unlike Schickel, Kroll praised Nichols for concentrating on a film about the American working class, rather than the topic of nuclear problems. Nichols was "masterly in creating the atmosphere of the plant. He shows working stiffs with dirty jobs, beer drinking, belches and double shifts, pain and humor."

Kroll also differed from Schickel in his assessment of Meryl's performance. "Meryl Streep's brilliant characterization of Silkwood," continued Kroll, "shows us a smart, sensitive woman with the constant jitters that comes from deep frustration. Streep turns a pain-in-the-ass into a complicated human being." Kroll was equally impressed with the other principal characters. "Russell is tender and decent and a man who can't handle the complications of love and nuclear power." He called Cher's performance her best work yet as a dramatic actress" and assessed the cast as "the best ensemble company of the year." Kroll had no difficulty accepting the motivation that Nichols presented for Karen. It was the "most basic and intimate question of personal survival. Her involvement forces deep sophistication. With great tension and suspense, it shows the atmosphere of fatality that hangs over everyone."

John Simon for the *New Yorker* considered the film an "absorbing but cloudy and unfocused account." He viewed it as "a passive advocacy film permeated with paranoia and hopelessness." If Simon had reservations about the film, he had none concerning Meryl's performance. "As the heroine, Meryl Streep has the external details of 'Okey bad girl' down pat. She makes the audience care deeply about Karen in a moving performance. More than any other actress today Streep is a master at making dramatic physical changes. As her health deteriorates, Streep changes from a carefree, fun-loving woman into a pale, thin, totally convincing bundle of nerves. In her final moments, Streep conveys the anguish of complete isolation."

More than any other critic, Simon focused on the lifestyle that Nichols created for Karen Silkwood. "Rather than illustrate a thesis or engage in political grandstanding, Nichols and the cast created a whole way of life." This appreciation of the talents of the director and the cast did not prevent Simon from commenting on his perception of the case presented in the film. Karen Silkwood was a "selfish, ornery, sluttish woman" who spied to get evidence in revenge on the company. Only when contaminated herself did she investigate willful negligence. But the film was "delicate, beautifully acted and finally terrifying."

Vincent Canby of the *New York Times* was much impressed with the film, although he saw within it serious flaws. "Mike Nichols has directed a precisely visualized, highly emotional melodrama that's going to raise a lot of hackles. Though far from perfect, 'Silkwood' may be the most serious work Mr. Nichols has yet done in films. Perhaps for the first time in a popular movie has America's petrochemical nuclear landscape been dramatized and with such anger and compassion." Canby was enthralled by Meryl's performance: "'Silkwood' offers another stunning performance by Meryl Streep. Miss Streep looks to be on what the Las Vegas people call 'a roll.' Her portrait of the initially self-assured and free-living, then radicalized and, finally, terrified Karen Silkwood is unlike anything she's done to date, except in its intelligence. It's a brassy, profane, gum-chewing tour de force, as funny as it is moving."

But Canby was of mixed opinions about the film itself. "Mr. Nichols and his writers, Nora Ephron and Alice Arlen, have attempted to impose a shape on a real-life story that even as they present it, has no easily verifiable shape. The muddle of fact, fiction and speculation almost, though not quite, denies the artistry of all that's gone before. Mr. Nichols and his writers attempt to acknowledge most of the theories (about Karen Silkwood's life and death) and, in so doing end their film in utter confusion. However, until these closing scenes . . . 'Silkwood' is a very moving work about the raising of the consciousness of one woman of independence, guts and sensitivity." Although focusing upon Meryl, Canby also enjoyed the performances of Russell and Cher. "If Miss Streep was superb, Mr. Russell and Cher are very, very good. Mr. Russell has become a star with the looks of a leading man and the substance and wit of a character player. Whether or not Cher is a great actress, I'm still not sure, but . . . there's an honest, complex screen presence there." Another reviewer was more unequivocal about Cher, finding her a delightful surprise. Her rendition of Dolly was played with "ease and beguiling naturalness," demonstrating that she was much more than a "left-over pop queen."

American Film, the most respected review source in film journalism, added its praise to Meryl, not only for her role in *Silkwood*, but also as a paean to her entire career to date: "The center of attention should be Meryl Streep, who adds Karen Silkwood to her list of brilliantly riveting performances. By now, it's so commonplace to praise Streep that one wonders if she is simply incapable of making a wrong move or striking a false note."

Although *Silkwood* was a strong contender for the Academy Award, the competition made it easy to neglect the film, particularly in view of the sensitive nature of the plot. The film was considered too uncentered, and the Academy had trouble warming up to a woman as unstable and enigmatic as Karen Silkwood, even if the subject matter had an appeal to what has been referred to as "the last 4000 liberals in the United States,"[20] meaning the Academy. The five films nominated—*The Big Chill*, *The Dresser*, *The Right Stuff*, *Tender Mercies* and *Terms of Endearment*—were all strong contenders, calling upon the emotions of either "remembrance past," patriotism or personal trauma. To no one's surprise, Meryl was nominated for Best Actress for *Silkwood* because, as one pundit put it, "Meryl Streep, like Katherine Hepburn, will be nominated year after year, whether there is someone else and even when there is not."[21] Although Meryl had come to be regarded as someone who would be a perennial nominee, she had won the award in 1982 for *Sophie's Choice*, and it seemed unlikely that she would join the select company of those who had won the award two years in a row, as had Katherine Hepburn and Luise Rainer. The Board of Nominators also selected Jane Alexander (*Testament*), Shirley MacLaine (*Terms of Endearment*), Julie Walters (*Educating Rita*) and Debra Winger (*Terms of Endearment*). Shirley MacLaine was considered an odds-on favorite for her portrayal of Aurora Greenway in *Terms of Endearment*. Despite being passed over for Best Picture, *Silkwood* garnered nominations in the other major categories: Mike Nichols for Best Director, Nora Ephron and Alice Arlen for Best Original Screenplay and Cher for Best Supporting Actress.

The ceremony itself should have won an award; at three hours and forty-six minutes, it was the longest ceremony in the history of the Academy.

When the marathon finally ended, Shirley MacLaine lived up to everyone's predictions by winning Best Actress. *Silkwood* was aced out of all the awards for which it had been nominated. James Brooks won Best Director for *Terms of Endearment*. Diminutive Linda Hunt received best supporting actress for her role as the male dwarf photographer in *The Year of Living Dangerously*.

For Meryl, it was perhaps best that she did not win; now she would have the time to devote to Don, Henry—and the newest member of the Gummer family.

12
Magic Meryl

Mary Willa Gummer, nicknamed "Mamie," was born in July 1983. Although she tried to keep it a secret, Meryl was six months pregnant at the Academy Awards ceremony. Meryl, Don and Henry had stayed with Cher during the ceremony, and Cher aided in the deception by draping Meryl in a loose-fitting Sonia Rykiel gown, one of Meryl's infrequent concessions to Cher's sartorial extravagances. Later, Cher gave Meryl a baby shower, presenting her with needlepointed lacy blue and pink pillows (made by Cher) with music boxes inside each. It was a quality of Meryl's affirmation of the future of the world that she got pregnant again. "She was hoping to keep it a secret a little while longer," said a friend, "but her radiance gave her away."[1]

Meryl decided to take a year off from her career to devote time to Don and her two children. "I *had* to take time out to have a baby," Meryl explained. "I just couldn't have balanced it all physically. Motherhood has a very humanizing effect. Everything gets reduced to essentials."[2] Many of her friends and colleagues in the film industry were surprised, considering the box-office and critical success of *Silkwood*. When asked about it in an interview, Meryl was quick to defend her decision. "Successful women are people whose life has more of an ebb and flow to it. It's certainly true of me. I have this period of great activity, and then I pull away. It isn't because my interest wanes. It's because it's necessary. Actually, I don't think I *could* work on a film now. I did that when I had my son and I absolutely don't know how I did it."[3]

Meryl was in mental anguish while she was carrying Mary. Her doctor had told he that he had detected an arrhythmic heartbeat in the fetus. Although in 60 percent of such cases the condition disappears at birth, Meryl was terrified. "You have no idea how scared I was," Meryl recalled. "I said, 'Well, what if the baby falls into the 40 percent, does that mean she'll have severe cardiac disease?' We worried about that right up until we went into the delivery room. We even had an infant cardiologist on standby during the birth."[4]

Immediately after the birth, Mary was put into an intensive-care unit. But Mary was born perfectly normal, and she was brought home within a few days. What Meryl remembers most clearly about that time was the agony of seeing her baby in the glass-enclosed cubicle, where she could not comfort her. "To see those monitor wires taped, two on the chest, two on her thighs . . . there's something horrifying about seeing your child all wired up and in a box, waiting for human contact. You just feel a newborn should never be out of your arms."[5]

After such a frightening experience, Meryl was more determined than ever to stay home with Don and the children. Don would work on his sculpture in his loft studio, and Meryl continued to review scripts and to make private investments in business ventures in her office at the apartment. Both Meryl and Don took an active interest in the care of the children, with Don taking Henry to school in the morning, and Meryl picking him up in the afternoon. And there were more frequent trips to the Christmas tree farm in Duchess County.

This was the kind of regimen that Meryl had come to realize was necessary to maintain an equilibrium in her life, and balance her personal and professional life. "Don and I are a lot alike," Meryl said recently. "He's a hermit and so am I. We like to be alone — with each other and our kids. We don't like the razzmatazz, the photographers and the glitz. We hardly ever go to Broadway openings because of all that. Some of our happiest times are when we're alone together in our place in the country."[6]

Meryl and Don are more determined than ever to not let Meryl's fame intrude into the children's lives. They acknowledge, however, that they cannot shield the children forever. "My kids are going to have it tough, because I'm famous," Meryl admits. "I have to talk to somebody who's famous and whose kids have grown up and been happy about it."[7]

Now that she had a daughter, Meryl was acutely aware of the pressures that Mary would face because she had a celebrity parent. "I hope she won't be inhibited by having what is perceived as a wildly successful mother. But she'll get a balanced picture. She'll see the glamour, but she'll also see me harassed, at the end of my rope."[8]

Eventually, Meryl had to return to the reality of getting on with her career, which caused her no little feelings of guilt. Fortunately, Meryl's next film was shot entirely in New York. In the fall of 1983, Michael Cristofer, who won a Pulitzer prize for the play *The Shadow Box*, contacted producer Marvin Worth about collaborating on a film about two people who reluctantly fall in love. After writing the screenplay, they sent it to Paramount after both 20th Century–Fox and Warner passed on it. Studio head Michael Eisner was lukewarm toward the project because he thought the plot too thin and doubted audiences would be interested in a love story that did not end up in bed.

Several junior executives at Paramount disagreed, and searched for some big box-office names to change Eisner's mind. For one thing, they perceived that the sexual permissiveness of the 1960s and 1970s was on the wane; people were starting to look for films with more traditional values. For another, they thought the very thinness of the plot would make it suffi- ciently flexible to appeal to a wide range of actors and actresses. They sent the script out simultaneously to ten actors and actresses, waiting to see who would express an interest in the roles. Jim Bridges, Robert Redford and Alan Alda all declined. The most enthusiastic response came from an unex- pected source: Robert De Niro, hardly known for his romantic leads.

Although scripts were sent to Jessica Lange, Jane Fonda and a number of other leading ladies, once De Niro was signed, the search began to center on Meryl. De Niro and Meryl had both wanted to reunite if the vehi- cle was right, and Paramount saw a box-office bonanza in recreating the electricity of *The Deer Hunter*. De Niro sent a copy of the script to Meryl, who quickly accepted his request that she co-star with him. De Niro also flexed his muscle in getting the studio to agree to hire Ulu Grosbard as director; he and Grosbard had formed a close personal and professional relationship on the set of *True Confessions*.

In order to interest Eisner, Worth and Cristofer asked De Niro and Meryl to improvise a script along the lines of how they envisioned their characters. When Eisner saw the new script, he became enthusiastic about the film and allocated a $13 million budget. Meryl and De Niro agreed to accept a substantially reduced salary, and filming got underway.

Falling in Love is about two prosperous Westchester commuters to New York, both comfortably married to dull partners, who reluctantly fall in love after a series of chance encounters on the train and in the city. Molly Gilmore (Meryl) is a commercial artist. Frank Raftis (De Niro) is an ar- chitectural engineer. In the first third of the film the audience sees them sitting near to, but not seeing, each other on the train. They telephone home from adjoining telephone booths, and they shop in the same stores, always oblivious of one another. Finally, at Christmastime, they literally run into each other at Rizzoli's, the fashionable bookstore. As they sort out dropped packages, they awkwardly begin talking, and they begin to sit together on the train. Their love affair begins through a series of shared lunches and visits to art galleries. Although they nervously try to avoid be- ing attracted to each other, they are drawn together in a guilt-ridden tryst that is never consummated.

Molly and Frank are both decent, honest people who are emotionally distraught over their nonsexual infidelity. Each confesses to a close friend: Molly to her sexually liberated colleague, Isabelle (Dianne Wiest), and Frank to drinking buddy Ed (Harvey Keitel). A sense of honor compels Molly and Frank to reveal the "affair" to their respective spouses. Molly's husband, Brian (David Clennon), is a physician preoccupied with his prac- tice, and Frank's wife, Ann (Jane Kaczmarek), is sweet, but distant. The marriages break apart, but Frank and Molly are too overcome with guilt to form their own union; they eventually go their separate ways. At the end

Molly (Streep) and Frank (Robert De Niro) may be crazy about each other, but the critics didn't love them back in Falling in Love.

of the film, they accidentally meet again at Christmas at Rizzoli's. They begin seeing each other again, but it is unclear whether they will let their feelings evolve into marriage.

Falling in Love was a deliberate envoking of the romantic films of the 1930s and 1940s, particularly *Brief Encounter*, the 1946 British film of the two star-crossed lovers which starred Celia Johnson and Trevor Howard. There is always the risk of trying to revive the ambiance of earlier films; the plot may appear hackneyed and dated to modern audiences. Grosbard, Meryl and De Niro were anxious to dispel that impression in prerelease publicity, striving to indicate the film's timely appeal to 1980s audiences.

"It's so old-fashioned, it's new," argued Ulu Grosbard. "I've done the people-undressing scene, you know. You get bored by it."[9]

Meryl was particularly concerned that contemporary films had come to equate sex with romance. "It's very sweet to know what's inside people's hearts, instead of what's under their clothes, don't you think?" she told reporters. "We live in a jaded, nonromantic time. Anybody can make out, but not everybody can feel the real thing. What interested me in this movie was the delicacy of it, of the emotions and the events."[10] "That's the nice thing about it, the not consummating it part of it," added De Niro in the same interview. "That's the whole point. Sex in a movie, isn't that the easy thing to do?"[11]

The urgency with which the director and the two stars reiterated the theme of sex-as-cliché in most movies, and the fresh approach that *Falling in Love* brought to modern films, sounded somewhat forced and underscored the continuing doubts of the producers, director and stars as to the reception that *Falling* would have from movie audiences. The roles of Molly and Frank were radically different from the characters in both Meryl and De Niro's recent films. Molly lacked the sultry allure of Sarah Woodruff and Sophie, and the frank sexuality of Karen Silkwood. Meryl tried to describe the emotions that she sought to create for Molly: "It has something to do with what happens to you the first time in the sixth grade. That's when it happened to me. You turn a corner and you expect to see him—that kind of little bitty thing. Something that makes you blush. Passion makes you that innocent again. We all know marriages where we say, 'What the hell does she see in him?' And with others we say: 'If I could only be like that,' and boom—they're divorced! There's a corner of their lives that's just waiting. And you don't even know it's waiting until it happens."[12]

There was particular concern by all involved that the public, so accustomed to seeing De Niro in offbeat, neurotic roles, such as the antisocial veteran of *Taxi Driver* or the amoral gangster in *Once Upon a Time in America*, would not accept him as a demure suburbanite. De Niro sought to dispel this doubt, saying, "My concern was that there should be tenderness and other things that come with love, and not just grabbing and groping. What interested me is the possibility of people meeting who have normal lives—whatever that is—and who weren't looking for anything. It was just a matter of chance."[13] Grosbard defended selecting De Niro for a role so out of character from his previous films: "I think it shows a side of Bobby he's never shown—tender, open, understanding and humorous. It's a high-risk part for a high-risk actor. I mean the ordinariness of it, and the fact that the character is working on such a small emotional level."[14]

The difficulty of the two roles was to make the awkwardness of Molly and Frank endearing to the audience, to evoke sympathy for the moral and emotional torment each feels as the affair progresses. It would have been impossible without the close friendship and mutual professional respect that De Niro and Meryl felt for each other. They had to improvise virtually all of the dialogue between Molly and Frank, beginning with the marathon sessions between the two in December 1983 and January 1984 several weeks before filming began. Whenever the threadbare plot of the script seemed not to work, Grosbard had such respect for the stars' professionalism that he would leave the two alone on the set to work out the kinks on their own. The two artists developed a kind of love for each other as the filming schedule wound down. "He's incapable of making a false move," said Meryl. "So when there's something wrong with the writing, he just can't do it. Then everyone realizes the scene's wrong and we fix it. He's infallible, like a compass. You're never adrift."[15] De Niro was equally impressed with his co-star, calling Meryl a "pure actress" with "many more colors than people have seen. She's a great comedienne."[16]

Perhaps the almost strident defense of the film by the stars and their director was a premonition of the critical reception of the film, which was devastating. Most of the critics bemoaned the wasting of two superior talents in such a formless, hokey film. The similarity to *Brief Encounter* was irritatingly transparent to reviewers. At least in the earlier film, the lovers were vibrant, sensitive people; Molly and Frank are virtually inarticulate and such bland people that the critics could muster little sympathy for their supposed suffering. Apparently, Meryl and De Niro had been *too* effective in trying to make Molly and Frank's lives ordinary.

Pauline Kael posed the question: "Can a vacuum love another vacuum?" She saw no reason for the two lovers to be even remotely attracted to each other. "The most compelling thing about them is the beauty-spot wart on De Niro's cheekbone; it has three dimensions—one more than anything else in the movie." Kael sympathized with a desire to resurrect the magic of the old romantic films of the thirties and forties, but saw nothing fresh; only the same, time-worn clichés. In one scene, Meryl is so nervous at an upcoming luncheon date with Frank that she tries on one outfit after another, each less satisfactory than the one before, until she finally ends up wearing her original outfit. *Falling* also had the predictable best friend–confidante for both Molly and Frank in order to convey to the audience the lovers' agony.

While she was disappointed in the script, Kael was generous to Meryl and De Niro's attempt to make something of the almost plotless story. "De Niro appears to be alert and ready to do something, but the inanity seems to be worse on him than on Streep, who stays fine-tuned, as if she really thought she was in a movie. The purpose of the techniques of naturalistic acting that they have been trained for is the inner emotions to be expressed in the external gestures. . . . Here is a parody of naturalistic acting—it's all externals."

Jack Kroll was kinder to both film and stars in his assessment. "The charm of this film is in its refusal to fall back on the old formulas, either romantic or realistic. This may be the only love story in which the climactic scene is a ferocious nonconsummation between lovers who want something besides the big bang." To Kroll, it was the chemistry between Meryl and De Niro, each of whom brought their own unique quirks of characterization to their roles of Molly and Frank that makes the film work. "Streep and De Niro create an adorable clustered energy; their interlocking rhythms are beautiful to behold. They make desire funny and they capture the anguish of virtuous people whose passion keeps bumping into their sense of honor. Only De Niro and Streep could have embodied so vividly the current state of passion—tentative, jittery, hungry as ever but chomping on emotional fast food."

Stanley Kauffmann chose to ignore the insubstantial plot in favor of extolling the acting of Meryl and De Niro. "The best passages of dialogue are those that, apparently (Cristofer) didn't write—the imprecise, half-expressed fumblings at tense moments that the leading actors improvised." In Kauffmann's estimation, the worst sin in the film was the waste of such enormous talent. "Streep summons no less nuance and subtlety than she would have done for a fresh, complex character. The result is not overload but verity. De Niro, dealing with an equally stock character, works equally to realize it as if it had never before been seen. What a waste of talent. But what talents."

David Denby's review, however, was more typical. "*Falling in Love* . . . is another nail in the coffin of American screenwriting. There *isn't* any screenplay here. These two are not looking for pleasure or excitement or romance, and neither, alas, is the movie. Like an awkwardly literal-minded person who won't stop talking, *Falling in Love* relentlessly pursues the moral ramifications of its not very interesting subject."

Nor was Denby any kinder to the characters portrayed by Meryl and De Niro. "Vibrating with guilt, honor, and fear right down to their last nerve ends, our heroes literally cannot formulate a sentence. As written, both charcters are ciphers. They are people without idiosyncrasies or jokes or obsessions, people with nothing on their minds. De Niro, for instance, can't find anything to play in this solid-citizen businessman–architect, and he goes flat . . . without his rage, his mockery and anguish, De Niro is merely empty. Meryl Streep, at least, looks right as a Westchester housewife who dabbles in commercial art. But since nothing has been written for her, she has to create a character out of bewilderment and indecision, ducking her head, smiling nervously, looking De Niro in the eyes and then looking away again, and on and on, through one scene after another. Streep fumbles beautifully; her incredibly mobile face reveals every hidden desire, every fear and evasion. But the character has been so impersonally conceived that her work comes off as an advanced-acting exercise. Streep the technician has never been more brilliant, but it's a meaningless performance. What is the use of putting these high-powered actors in nothing? The filmmakers have nothing to give us but dreary upper-middle-class naturalism and fine moral sentiments."

Richard Schickel of *Time* was more succinct, but just as unimpressed. "The suspense, for the viewer, is not exactly killing. Neither is the wit of the dialogue. . . . It generally consists of inarticulate expressions of desire and feeble excuses for not consummating it. . . . De Niro's performance consists mostly of doleful looks, Streep's of brushing back her hair and giving two vigorous nods whenever she tells a lie, and that says it all about Ulu Grosbard's lugubrious direction."

Vincent Canby of the *The New York Times* did not find the movie poorly done, merely trite and unworthy of the acting talents of the leading actors. "'Falling in Love' is not a bad movie by any means. It's not stupid, or gross or cheap. It's been done with taste, but it's the sort of production that, even when it works, which it frequently does, seems too small and trite to have had so much care taken on it. What keeps the movie going is its combination of intelligent performances and expert timing. . . . When the characters are allowed to become at least partially articulate, their emotions carry real impact. There's also one quite wonderful love scene, which may mark a breakthrough for love scenes in this day and age, though not for reasons one would expect. It's at such moments that one realizes the kind of romantic comedy 'Falling in Love' might have been instead of the high-toned soap opera it seems content to be."

Even an actress of the caliber of Meryl Streep can be expected to make a poor film occasionally, although a series of them could quickly make her box-office poison. But a remarkable feature of Meryl's career is her uncanny ability to follow such a role with a truly outstanding one, as in *Silkwood* after the disastrous *Still of the Night*. Meryl found such a role in *Plenty*, the film adaptation of David Hare's play. Within weeks of finishing *Falling in Love*, Meryl went to London to begin filming with the inimitable Sir John Gielgud; this time Don, Henry and Mary went with her.

The protagonist of *Plenty* is Susan Traherne (Meryl), whose work in the French Resistance during World War II proves to be the idealistic high point of her life. Nothing in her subsequent life carries the emotional intensity of that time, and she leads an increasingly frustrated existence in trying to recapture that sense of commitment and meaning.

After the war, Susan goes to England and marries a successful British diplomat (Charles Dance). But she becomes disgusted at the superficiality and deceit inherent in the diplomatic corps, and becomes a shrill critic of postwar Britain in particular, and the world in general. She effectively ruins her husband's career by such outspoken criticism, particularly to his immediate superiors (Ian McKellan and John Gielgud).

Although Susan is fearless in her strident criticism of virtually everything and everyone around her in a selfish and self-absorbed manner, she is bound by her own inability to effect change in her life, as well as by the societal constraints upon women in the 1950s. Consequently, she does nothing to realize her frustrated idealism. Eventually, she deserts her husband and suffers a nervous breakdown. The film ends with a pathetically whimsical Susan reminiscing about the first rush of youthful idealism she felt as a teenager in France shortly after the Allies liberated it; it was a vision that tormented her for the rest of her life and ultimately destroyed her.

Susan Traherne is one of the most powerful roles in modern theatre, and director Fred Schepisi and Meryl were determined that it would translate well from the stage to the screen. Meryl took pains to explain her perception of the role to reporters on the set. "Playing a character as I am, who is uncompromising in the demands she makes on herself and on other people, I really have to come up to that challenge, and it tests my mettle. When the stakes are so high, when everything is a matter of life or death, and you don't know if you're going to see each other the next day or not, or if there's *going* to be a next day, I think that life has richness and things *matter*."[17]

The role required a strong and unusual woman, just the type of character that Meryl had made her trademark. "I loved her anger and the size of it," she continued, "and her fearlessness in expressing it. And I also was attracted by the dream inside of her, and the idealism. To me, she seemed like someone who all through her life up to middle age just doesn't stop being as altruistic as only teenagers are, and obnoxious about the purity of her opinions and what she demands of the world. I think we've seen a lot of heroes in literature and in drama, men who ask a lot of their circumstances, and of society and the world, and who are demanding, aggressively so. I don't think that's unusual; what I think is unusual is that it's a woman."[18]

Rather than exploit the mannerisms that had characterized her earlier roles, Meryl was more restrained as she sought to focus attention upon the difficult choices facing Susan—whether to accept passively the postwar hypocrisies and banality that she sees all around her, or to speak out caustically in a manner that will destroy both her marriage and her social position. Meryl was also under tremendous pressure in playing opposite John Gielgud in two extended scenes. Gielgud had the terrifying reputation of ruthlessly stealing scenes by such subtle means as a slight pause, a wry smile or an arched eyebrow; it had overshadowed more than one costar's performance, virtually to the point of obscurity.

Gielgud did shamelessly steal the thunder of those scenes, but he developed an unqualified admiration of Meryl's talent and poise. "She seemed completely in control of her emotions, pace and timing, and in her reactions to other people," he would say later. "It was remarkable. I was enormously impressed by that."[19]

Once again, Meryl had to master a foreign accent; she wanted her

Top: Streep as Susan Traherne in Plenty. *Bottom: Susan Traherne with friends of the Resistance, including Alice Park (Tracey Ullman, background center), and diplomat Raymond Brock (Charles Dance, far right).*

aristocratic English to be impeccable, especially when playing opposite Gielgud, the quintessential Shakespearean actor. "If I think about the word, I'm lost," she sighed, recalling the times when she was less than successful in disguising her American accent. "I just have to think about why I am saying what I want to say, and hope it comes out right. Sometimes it doesn't and the sound man comes over and says, 'Very, very New Jersey.'"[20]

One method that Meryl developed for coping with the tension was to attend the screening of each day's shooting. "I go to rushes because they have wine and potato chips at rushes," she explains. "I'm so tired at the end of the day, it's like a little reward for me to go to rushes. To shoot a movie twelve to fourteen hours a day, and go home and wonder what it is that you've done is excruciating. I just need to know what it looks like. It's like painting blindfolded."[21]

Just as filming was ending and Meryl was preparing to return to the United States, Robert De Niro visited her at her hotel. Rumors leaked to the press that they were discussing yet another film project, perhaps a comedy, but neither was willing to talk to reporters about it until their plans had solidified.

Plenty received favorable critical attention upon its release in the summer of 1985. *Newsweek*'s David Ansen stated: "It's a safe bet that the movie version of David Hare's *Plenty* waves the red flag of ambiguity. It's *designed* to exact an ambivalent response to its heroine, Susan Traherne, whom some will see as a brave soul, and some as a madwoman." He described Susan as "angry, idealistic, neurotic, imperious . . . a loud and increasingly unstable critic. Susan is not some pure uncorruptible soul. What makes her exasperating is her refusal to actually *do* anything about her discontent. Much as we want to embrace her idealism, we can't deny that she's a selfish, self-absorbed scold, as much a product of her time as its victim. Unable to change the world, she acts out her disdain in destructive outbursts." In praising this "highly literate, fragmented epic," Ansen gave kudos to Ian Baker's cinematography, Richard MacDonald for his production design and Bruce Smeaton's score, but reserved his highest accolades for "a sterling cast, dominated by Streep's daring and splendid performance. Her very first scenes as a young woman seem far too brittle and edgy, but there is little else to quarrel with." He was also impressed with Charles Dance as Susan's husband, Tracey Ullman as Traherne's bohemian friend Alice, Sting as the would-be father of Susan's child, and, of course, John Gielgud, whom Ansen found to be "at his best as the diplomat Darwin." Ian McKellan, portraying another senior diplomat, "has one stunning scene as the smooth spokesman for the establishment Susan despises." In Ansen's estimation, "*Plenty* can be argued with both as a political and esthetic object, but it's not lightly shaken off."

In characterizing Susan Traherne, Richard Corliss of *Time* called her "part Joan of Archetype, part loony from Loonyville—a bitter romantic who never got over her teenage crush on reckless idealism . . . . Even when Susan is not quite explicable or sympathetic, she is a compelling spectacle, turning heads and stomachs with her coruscating monologues." As with her other heroines, Meryl sought to portray a woman with character flaws, but appealing ones that could evoke the audience's sympathy. As far as Corliss was concerned, she succeeded admirably. "As the frustrated houswife with bloody *nothing* to do, Streep gives her fiercest, most controlled perform-ance since *The French Lieutenant's Woman*. . . . When embarrassed, she flushes; when attacked, she shoots back a laser-like stare; when deter-mined to be aroused, she looks carnivorous. She radiates the odd pleasure Susan takes in being thought dangerous—if women cannot be taken seriously, at least they can be feared. With *Plenty*, Streep was granted the luxury of a character with surprising edges and dark corners."

As fond as Stanley Kauffmann is of Meryl, he found both the film and her performance flawed. He considered the weaknesses of the play to have been transferred to the screen: As intelligent as Susan is, she should have been able to grasp that wars are never followed by the period of idealism that sustains those who fought it, and Hare's radical condemnation of "a self-gratifying society and a stodgy government" lacks conviction and focus. "Susan seems even more ethically and intellectually slothful, a woman waiting for the good *not* to happen, so that she can take refuge first in bitterness, then in recurrent 'mental' episodes. She looks down disdain-fully from unearned elevation. This makes the film sentimental, where the play, though flawed, was not."

In turning to Meryl's performance, Kauffmann found similar disap-pointment. "I've been fervent about her since her drama school days, but I think her performance here—excepting *Still of the Night*, which was just a blip on the screen for all concerned—is her least successful film work to date." The anxiety that Meryl felt in being surrounded by masters of the Shakespearan stage, with their vocal richness, proved to be justified; it was the central point around which Kauffmann formed his critical judgment. "Her voice sounds limited, uninflected, insufficiently interesting. . . . Here she is surrounded by English actors brought up in a tradition where the voice is not just a means of making words audible but is the instrument with which acting begins . . . . All of them, merely by using their techniques truthfully, make Streep sound vocally lackluster. She seems here so con-cerned about merely sounding English that it absorbs much of her imag-inative energy." For once, Meryl's talents of accents and mimicry, which had been the wonder of her directors, colleagues and audiences, had ap-parently failed her.

Marcia Pally, writing for the prestigious *Film Comment*, was en-thralled with *Plenty*, and with Meryl. Carefully comparing the play to the film version, she found that "It's a successful effort in spite of significant

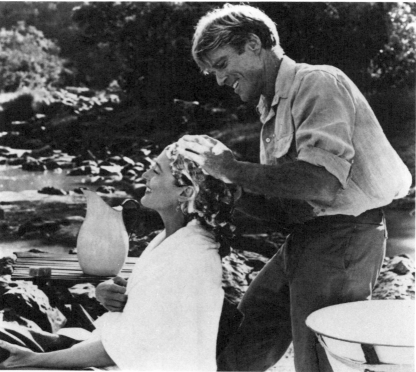

Top: Meryl Streep as Karen in Out of Africa. *Bottom: Denys (Robert Redford) washes Karen's hair after a long safari in* Out of Africa.

changes. Fred Schepisi (along with director of photography Ian Baker) turned in a detailed and elegant *Plenty*." Turning to Meryl's performance, Pally wrote: "During all these ups and downs, Streep never becomes maudlin or predictable. Rebellious at one point, acid or even pathetic at another, she keeps turning her character over, exploring Susan's attempts to grapple with her surroundings. . . . Her contained interpretation stands up well under the scrutiny of the camera and saves Streep from the mannerisms that have marred her other roles."

Plenty was released within weeks of three other films that portrayed heroines who are faced with difficult choices and who choose the paths of passion and intelligence, even though it leads them into areas that traditionally exclude women; if they dare presume to enter, they suffer the denial of the protective mantle of being a "lady." In addition to Meryl's role in *Plenty*, Jessica Lange portrayed the earthy 1960s country singer Patsy Kline in *Sweet Dreams*; Sissy Spacek appeared as the whistle-blower in Tennessee governor Ray Blanton's administration in *Marie* and Glenn Close was a crusading attorney in *Jagged Edge*. Critics were already predicting that Streep, Lange, Spacek and Close would be the nominees for Best Actress for 1985.

Shortly after returning to New York, Meryl signed to appear opposite Robert Redford — Hollywood's unofficial indication that an actress had attained superstardom — in a film adaptation of Isak Dinesen's *Out of Africa*. Meryl is Karen Blixen (Dinesen's real name), a woman who, in turn-of-the-century Africa, dared to buck the restrictions of a male-dominated society, and suffered for her choice.

The logistics of filming Dinesen's 1937 memoir of her seventeen-year experience in Africa had stymied director Sidney Pollack for twelve years. The sprawling story lacked focus until five books on Blixen and her lover, Denys Finch-Hatton, reawakened public interest in them. At last Pollack had an angle to interest Hollywood producers — a love story. Blixen's love affair with Finch-Hatton had been a relatively small part of her memoir, but journalist Kurt Luedtke wrote a screenplay built around their affair. Luedtke is a self-described "hopeless Meryl Streep fan"[22] and tailored the script to suit her unique acting style. Pollack suggested Robert Redford to play Finch-Hatton, but Leudtke objected. "I didn't think the role was big enough for him," he explains.[23] It took a call from Universal Studio president Frank Price, who insisted on Redford, to change his mind.

Out of Africa is the story of an indominatable woman who will not compromise her principles nor succumb to the harsh elements, but who was willing to forsake everything she had built over seventeen years of unrelenting struggle for the love of an extraordinary man. Karen Dinesen (Meryl) is a member of pre–World War I Danish aristocracy, engaged to Baron von Blixen. She breaks the engagement at a shooting party when she learns of his repeated infidelities, then abruptly accepts the proposal of

Bror von Blixen (Klaus Maria Brandauer), the Baron's brother. Bror and Karen leave for Kenya, where he has bought land for a coffee plantation.

Karen initially finds the adjustment from aristocrat to pioneer a difficult one. The arid land requires constant irrigation to make it suitable for coffee plants, and tribal elders resist her efforts to establish a school for the local native children. Before the first crop can be harvested, World War I breaks out in Europe. The British settlers form a militia to stop a German advance against Kenya, and Bror volunteers. He has become disenchanted with the plantation and bored with his marriage. Although she has no love for Bror, Karen feels a marital obligation to him, and their parting is an awkward one.

Determined to make the plantation successful, Karen suffers prejudice in the male-dominated society for "unsexing" herself by insisting on doing "man's work." Her one ally is a free-spirited safari guide, Denys Finch-Hatton (Robert Redford). They meet at a New Year's Eve party in 1914, where they are attracted to each other. Denys frequents the plantation between safaris, encouraging her independence. They become lovers cautiously; she feels guilty committing adultery, and he is a fiercely independent man who will not accept the constraints of marriage.

Bror returns to the plantation, but only to tell Karen that he wants a divorce, and leaves to live in town with his mistress. Karen presses Denys for marriage, but finds he is pulling farther away from her the more insistent she becomes; eventually, he leaves her for a less-demanding woman.

Abandoned by both husband and lover, the final blow comes with the destruction of the coffee crop due to drought. Karen decides to sell the plantation, but her tenacity has earned her the respect of the settlers and natives alike, and they bid her a farewell tribute, each in their own way; the natives by continuing her school, and the colonials by allowing her the rare honor of a drink in the all-male club bar.

The night before she is to leave by train for Nairobi, Denys reappears. He confesses he cannot return to his former lifestyle without her and proposes. He flies off at dawn in his private plane, promising to return on Friday; later that week, Karen receives the stunning news that he was killed in an airplane crash. She delivers a touching tribute at his funeral, then leaves Kenya for Denmark, never to return. The film ends with the narration of an elderly Karen recalling her days in Africa, as the scene reveals lions lying on her beloved Denys' grave overlooking the Serengheti plain.

The cast assembled in Nairobi, Kenya, in January 1985 to begin four and a half months of location shooting. Both Redford and Meryl brought their families, and they settled in rented houses in a Nairobi suburb within blocks of each other. Director Sydney Pollack had to contend with a myriad of seemingly insurmountable problems: torrential rains that caused weeks of delay, arranging safaris into the interior, wild animals roaming

Top: Karen (Streep) tends Kamante's (Joseph Thiaka) leg as Farah (Malick Bowens) looks on. Bottom: Providing medical attention for the Kikuyu living on her farm.

onto the set and the demands of the 100-man production crew and 10,000 extras hired from nearby Maasai and Kikuyu tribes.

Pollack was surprised by the one problem he did *not* have: egotism from his two megastars. Neither brought a retinue to look after him or her, a fact much appreciated by the crew. Redford, who craves privacy, bore with equanimity the attentions of curious fans as he waited for his luggage in the Nairobi airport. Meryl came prepared to work, establishing a reputation for being among the first on the set every morning. Redford and Meryl each admired the other's professionalism, which could account for the ease of their relationship on the set, but Redford offered another explanation. "I'm very shy and Meryl's very shy," he told reporters.[24] It was a mutual respect for the other's sensitivity that formed a close personal bond on the set.

Another reason for a lack of tension during the grinding months of filming was Redford's sense of humor and his ability to crack up the cast and crew at any moment. Mike Bugara, a Kenyan actor who portrays one of Karen's servants, recalls a frustrating scene in which he could not spill a bottle of wine correctly on Meryl and Redford. "I was so nervous working with Redford that I spilled the wine wrong six times. I finally got it right by actually dropping the bottle. Everyone, including Redford, laughed and clapped."[25] On another occasion, Redford strode onto the set, slapped an open peanut butter sandwich into Pollack's hand, then proceeded to play an intensely dramatic scene while the crew had to stifle their guffaws. The crew was surprised to find a superstar of Redford's stature so unselfconscious about his celebrity status; he preferred to talk about archaeology, especially his preoccupation with Stonehenge.

The cast and crew were no less impressed with Meryl. As assistant director Terence Clegg remembers, "She's a superb pro. She's never late. She knows every line. She's an absolute sweetheart. There was no drama, no star temperament."[26] On one occasion, Meryl endeared herself to several of the elderly women serving as extras by distributing her shawls to them during the cool evening shots.

The only source of discord occurred over animal trainer Hubert Wells' protest against riflemen on the set prepared to shoot his lions if one made a menacing move toward the actors, but Clegg and Pollack had no intention of letting their superstars be mauled. Meryl quickly learned the risk of location filming in Africa. "Every morning at 5 a.m. the lions would wake up," she recalls. "The first time it happened I thought someone was dying in the house next door. I shook my husband and said 'Don, Don, something terrible's happening.'"[27] She eventually became so confident that she took to walking across the game reserve, until one of the crew raced up in a jeep to remind her that the leopards still had fangs and claws, whereupon Meryl immediately jumped into the jeep. Redford took it upon himself to make nightly rounds to ensure that everyone's tent was zipped up tight when they had to camp out on the plain for a safari scene.

The months of filming had their moments of irony and humor, as when the coffee beans stubbornly refused to blossom, requiring cast and crew to decorate each plant with tufts of shaving cream to simulate blossoms. More serious were the charges of racism by the Kenyan government because white extras were earning twice as much as African extras (the wages were quickly equalled). The Kenyan press kept up a tirade against the film, accusing the production company of glorifying colonialism by espousing Dinesen's "outright racist" attitudes toward Africa.

But, apart from these minor problems, filming went well, with the filming coming in under budget at $30 million. Not surprisingly, Meryl once again left location a friend of virtually everyone on the set. She continued to keep her promise to treat even the bit players with the same concern and respect Jane Fonda had shown her in *Julia*. "Meryl always made me feel comfortable," says Mike Bugara. "She'd give me big hug and kiss."[28]

One unexpected benefit from the months on location in Africa was a fresh, innovative approach to Don's work. During filming, he developed an interest in painting watercolors with African motifs that intrigued both his dealer and art patrons when they were exhibited in New York.

Critics were divided between admiration of yet another foreign language accent (Danish) flawlessly mastered by Meryl and dissatisfaction at Pollack's emphasis on costume and spectacular scenery at the expense of his talented stars. Molly Haskell, writing for *Ms.*, found Redford "miscast but nevertheless charming," and applauded Meryl and Redford's decision not to let their on-screen love affair be conveyed in "cuddly" scenes, but rather "to say a great many things with very few words." She credits Meryl with coming "as close as anyone is likely to come to embodying at least some of the puzzling and fascinating facets of Karen Blixen." But in the final analysis, Haskell found Meryl's performance sadly off the mark. "There's something solid and un-chameleonlike about her that prevents her from inhabiting the volatile and ascetic Dinesen. There's a fundamental, tempermental clash: Streep's ego (and genius) as an actress is to submit completely to another character; Dinesen's was to assert, rule, behave outrageously, in order to become, completely, herself. To portray her faithfully demands an act of exposure of which Streep, for all her talents, is incapable."

David Denby of *Newsweek* took the opposite point of view. "Streep and Dinesen are a match made in heaven: she slips into her Danish accent as if born to the role and captures the woman's courage, humor, vanity and elegance. . . . This is not just another exemplary woman from the New Hollywood feminist textbook, but a full-bodied *thinking* heroine we come to know and care about deeply." Denby had nothing but praise for the entire cast which "performs impeccably." Although the crux of the film is the love affair between Streep and Redford, Denby praised the interplay between Meryl and Klaus Maria Brandauer, calling their scenes together "little gems of intimate, chummy cynicism." While some critics believed Redford miscast as the Oxford-educated poet Denys Finch-Hatton, Denby credits him with a sophisticated understanding of the inner man. "Redford understands the character's dashing impenetrability.... He knows how to show the loneliness of a man everyone loves." But his highest praise was reserved for Meryl; after all, it was her movie from start to finish. "Streep's Karen ... is a complex and commanding woman.... At once haughty and playful, romantic and levelheaded ... Streep brings a teasing wit to her scenes with her servants that captures well the tensions in a woman who was both a master and a supplicant...." With such universally high praise for the ensemble, it is no surprise that Denby considered the film among the year's finest. "'Out of Africa' is a sprawling but always intelligent romantic epic ... [which] provides old-movie lushness and romance without ever underestimating its characters', or the audience's, intelligence."

   Time's Richard Schickel was more taciturn, but joined Denby in a favorable review of both the film and the performances of the entire cast. Redford successfully performs the somewhat mystical role that both Dinesen and Pollack intended Finch-Hatton to serve: a rapidly-vanishing symbol of the rugged individual in harmony with nature, "a stand in for the spirit of Africa. Laconic, ironic, elusive and, in his silky way, brutal, he continually offers his lover spectacular glimpses of a great nature." Schickel was even more impressed with Meryl's performance: "Streep, as Dinesen, is his perfect match. Always at her best when challenged to leave her own time and place for regions more passionate and generous, Streep embodies an aristocrat's arrogance toward the unknown and an artist's vulnerability to it." In his opinion, the film was an unqualified success in which the two stars interacted in a comfortable way devoid of any attempts at upstaging each other. "They play against each other warily and discreetly, often content to keep their silences, and let the flow of the movie itself, speak for them."

   Meryl's friends were surprised to find that she intended to start another film immediately upon her return to New York. Even while she was on location for *Out of Africa*, she began reading the script for *Heartburn*, based on Nora Ephron's caustic *roman à clef* about her divorce from Watergate reporter Carl Bernstein. It would give her the opportunity to work again with director Mike Nichols and co-star with Jack Nicholson. Most importantly, she could expand her already considerable film repertoire to include comedy. As soon as she returned to New York, she told Sam Cohn to sign her for the part of Rachel Samstat.

   Heartburn is the tragicomic story of the disintegration of a marriage. Rachel Samstat (Meryl) is a Jewish newspaper reporter who has survived

Meryl Streep and Jack Nicholson in a publicity photo for Heartburn.

one failed marriage and studiously shuns all involvement to avoid another. At the wedding of a friend, she meets Mark Forman (Jack Nicholson), a Washington columnist with a reputation for philandering and a broken marriage of his own. Rachel finds his eccentric charm irresistible, and she abandons her fears to rush into marriage after a week-long courtship. Even so, it takes entreaties from her father, friends, therapist and Mark himself to get her to leave the bedroom, where Rachel has barricaded herself in panic on her wedding day, to walk down the aisle.

At first, the marriage is idyllic, with Mark and Rachel exchanging affectionate protestations of love. But, slowly, little irritations appear: Mark's eccentricities, such as singing loudly at all times of the day and night, wear thin; Rachel's excessive angst at redecorating their Washington townhouse and her meticulous cleanliness infuriate him. Rachel seeks solace from her therapist (Maureen Stapleton), while Mark enlists the sympathy of their friends Arthur Siegel (Richard Masur) and his wife, Julie (Stockard Channing).

Irritations are placed aside with the birth of their son. Mark and

Rachel prove to be doting, overindulgent parents. But Mark soon grows weary of domestic bliss and gives in to his wandering eye. Pregnant once more, Rachel catches Mark in an affair. Humiliated, she returns to her father's apartment in New York, vowing never to see Mark again, only to sit by the telephone waiting for his call. When he comes to New York, full of contrition, Rachel returns with him to Washington. The marriage returns to an outward semblance of its former happiness, but Rachel's silent suspicions create tension which all of Mark's declarations of love and fidelity cannot dispel. Mark and Rachel are drawn together again at the birth of their second child, but it is only a brief interlude. A casual comment by Mark at a dinner party confirms Rachel's suspicions that he is philandering once more. She calmly dumps pasta on Mark's head and leaves. Rachel can no longer live a lie for the convenience and security of marriage. In the final scene, she boards a plan for New York with her two children.

Despite the somber tone of the ending, there are many affecting moments of humor as Rachel and Mark lurch their way through marriage, separation and divorce. Meryl handles these scenes with an adroit touch that reveals her previously untapped comedic talent. Nicholson plays Mark with his customary smooth arrogance and endearing charm. But his character is so one-dimensional that he is only a backdrop to Rachel; the movie is all Meryl, and she dominates it. As a result, there is very little chemistry between Meryl and Nicholson. Perhaps for this reason, she and Nicholson got along well and were comfortable in their scenes together, but their relationship lacked the camaraderie she had enjoyed with her other male co-stars.

With the exception of Pauline Kael, the critics virtually apologized for not liking *Heartburn*. *Time*'s Richard Corliss identified the most commonly recognized flaw in the film: the absence of any theme and the one-sided narrative that focuses upon Rachel's pain and leaves Mark a shallow cipher. "The viewer, who is vouchsafed all Rachel's perceptions and prejudices, is never told Mark's reasons for seeking solace in the bed of a society hostess while his wife is seven months pregnant." Corliss credits Meryl with another role of subtle gestures conveying a wealth of meaning in a movie that has no meaning to convey. She is superb in "confiding a querulous eyebrow or subtle grimace, simultaneously inhabiting and commenting on her role." He can only pity Nicholson, who appears in the film as "only half a man, all surface and no substance, and finally he distances himself from Mark, his face going slack in a kind of moral torpor."

David Ansen, in *Newsweek*, lavished praise upon Nichols' direction while lamenting that such a wealth of talent was wasted in a film of so little substance. "'Heartburn' evokes a happy marriage with such relaxed assurance that one barely notices the absence of plot." He agreed with Corliss that the fundamental weakness of the film lay in screenwriter Nora

Ephron's (who adapted her novel to the screen) lack of interest in delving into Mark's motives in cheating on his pregnant wife. "'Heartburn' isn't interested in answering these questions—it doesn't even ask them. It becomes just another generic story about a suffering wife. The frustration of 'Heartburn' is its triviality; it doesn't seem to be about anything." Ansen gives a short, obligatory mention of the stylish and creative work of both Meryl and Nicholson before returning to the essentially flawed nature of the film. "Yet for all the talent at work, the movie doesn't add up to much. . . . The movie works neither as a tragicomic love story nor as a revenge fantasy."

David Denby, writing for *New York*, echoed the general dissatisfaction of critics over the shallowness of Nicholson's role, but focused upon Nichols' genius at detail, calling him a "master of small, telling moments." He preferred to dwell upon Nichols' direction rather than the essentially empty roles of the stars; he dismissed Meryl's performance with a brief nod to the scene in which Nora rushes home from the beauty parlor to find evidence of Mark's infidelity, which Ansen called "wonderful and terrifying."

It fell to Stanley Kauffmann in *The New Republic*, and Pauline Kael in the *New Yorker* to bluntly call the film a failure. Kauffmann hinted that the reunion of Nichols, Ephron and Meryl (they had all worked together on *Silkwood*) may have allowed sentiment to get in the way of thinking about how to make a weak screenplay into an appealing film with a strong theme. He saw two major flaws in the film: weak, undefined characters and an absence of theme to hold the structure together. Essentially, Kauffmann found Nichols to be out of his depth. "He is one of the best of directors, on stage or screen, as long as he sticks to lightweight stuff." He believed that Nicholson was seriously miscast, but he found Meryl's performance to have "affecting joy, warmth and heartsickness," though suffering from "the lack of pungent characterization in the script." The most outstanding performance, in the opinion of Kauffmann and most critics, was the spoof of Alistair Cooke in a fantasy sequence adroitly played by English actor John Wood.

Pauline Kael praised the cast, but added that "after a while the scenes that don't point anywhere begin to add up, and you start asking yourself, 'What is this movie about?'" The fatal flaw was excising from the screenplay the Jewish humor that gave the novel its biting satire. Without that, according to Kael, Streep's Rachel is nothing more than a "joyless performance" and Nicholson's Mark a character "with nothing to do." In the end, such an undefined film becomes little more than "an assortment of moments, with nothing holding the moments together." *Heartburn* proved to be an artistic failure and a box-office flop for Meryl. Perhaps it is fortunate that she resolved early in her career to dismiss reviews and put the last project behind her in order to concentrate on the next one.

Shortly after filming ended for *Heartburn*, Meryl's friends understood why she had done three films back-to-back: She announced that she was pregnant once again. Grace Gummer was born in May 1986. Don and Meryl promptly nicknamed her "Gracie."

Now Meryl was content to retreat with her family to the rustic beauty of their Connecticut estate. Although the Gummers were sheltered from curious onlookers by an imposing stone wall and a twenty-acre lake, they refused to employ sophisticated security equipment or guards; they relied instead upon the civility of their neighbors to inhibit intrusions on their privacy. In fact, the 3800 people of Salisbury rarely take note of their local celebrity. In this farming community with no movie theatres and few televisions, there is little time or interest to gawk at megastars. Meryl is accepted as just another mother who shops with her children in town or cheers her son on the school hockey team.

Her anonymity suits Meryl fine. "I'd much prefer not to have all the attention and adulation, people going beserk when they see me in public," she insists. "Actually, I'm sort of boring, except for this incredibly fascinating career I have. Day to day, you know, I'm just like everybody else."[29] So concerned were the Gummers about their privacy that they moved completely out of New York, although they maintain an apartment on Central Park West where they stay on trips in Manhattan for a play or dinner.

But being out of the public eye periodically does not mean Meryl is out of its thoughts. In 1986, she received the People's Choice Award for favorite all-around female entertainer. While flattering, this excessive public adulation worries her because of the direction she would like her career to take. "The praise is nice, and being able to pick scripts is wonderful . . . but the extreme publicity has to create an expectation in an audience that I can't possibly satisfy."[30] Realizing that "leading lady" roles are available to actresses for only a limited time, Meryl prefers to accept more and more character parts that can remain her forte for the rest of her career, just as they have for Katharine Hepburn. Such roles also keep her close to the eclecticism of the theatre, which remains her first love. Consequently, the next script she accepted was *Ironweed*, based upon William Kennedy's bestselling novel. In that film, she and Jack Nicholson portray two down-and-out transients in Depression-era New Jersey. Meryl will once again forsake her classical beauty, appearing as a homely, middle-aged "bag lady."

But the roles of wife and mother are the most important to Meryl. Don often is overlooked in the rush of publicity and interviews. It would be understandable if he bridled at his own artistic creativity being buried in the avalanche of praise showered upon his wife. It is Don who must pick up and travel to her various film locations or act as single parent for weeks when her family cannot accompany Meryl. Such a situation has wrecked more than one Hollywood marriage, but Meryl has remained particularly sensitive, constantly poking fun at her celebrity status. "It has to be difficult for Don Gummer that all the attention is on his wife," observes Maureen Stapleton. "He handles it, but I think Meryl's attitude helps. She keeps things light, and I give her a lot of credit for that."[31] Meryl's own assessment of the success of their relationship focuses less on herself and more on their mutual respect for art and the circumstances under which they married. "I think one reason our marriage is working is that I didn't marry too early. Don knows all about my work and what it means to me, and I understand about his work. We both know what we can give and what we can take from each other."[32]

Balancing motherhood with a career frequently makes for a hectic private and professional life, but there is no doubt in Meryl's mind that it is worth it—or which would survive if she had to make a choice. "Being a housewife and mother is difficult," she says. "It's really a very, very difficult job, and I applaud anybody who comes through it unscathed."[33] But should the demands of her film career interfere with motherhood, she would devote the rest of her life "to give my children a good life, a happy life. Thank God I know who my real people are. My husband, my family. At home they know the real me—just plain old Meryl herself."[34]

13
Chameleon

Meryl Streep is now at the top of her profession, transcending even the title superstar into a new superlative: Megastar.　.

She is widely acknowledged as the most admired actress of her generation, and is the first choice of directors for every important female role available in films today. Why does Meryl Streep generate such enthusiasm, and how has she reached this pinnacle of success in just ten years?

She is a thoroughly skilled, highly intelligent actress who stirs excitement on the screen through a series of carefully selected roles that demonstrate her chameleon-like ability to adapt her malleable face, body and voice to any character with emotional conviction. Her ambivalent heroines have a social consciousness in her films, in which they display several emotions at once, allowing the audience to get a glimpse of the inner conflict they are undergoing.

Meryl also has an uncanny ability to easily create and portray any character with brilliance. She is staggeringly different in every role, whether the earthy Karen Silkwood, or the patrician Susan Traherne. Her capacity to bring to life such widely divergent characters is the result of a precise, detailed technique that encompasses the subtle nuances of her characters, causing one commentator to note her seemingly "effortless skills at stepping in and out of roles."[1] But it is an extraordinarily disciplined technique that demands perfection from each performance that another observer characterized as an "internal pressure, a dynamic defensiveness that spurs her to greatness while preventing the slightest slip into complacency."[2]

Meryl herself finds it difficult to articulate her concept of acting technique. "I don't have any method," she says. "People who have est, people who have other means of relaxation, feel they have 'The Way' tucked inside their scripts. I don't have that. I sort of go at everything from a different direction."[3] Her approach is to completely assume the life of the character she is portraying, to see the character's world and step into it.

Another reason for her highly successful career is a careful selection of quality productions with challenging roles that stimulate her considerable creativity. All of her films have been of high quality, and not always the most lucrative ones she could have chosen, preferring critical successes over just box office successes. One close friend commented, "Meryl's always had the courage of her convictions, and these convictions have always been dignified. I know about jobs she's turned down at times when it would have been nice for her to have done those things."[4]

Meryl admits that she is motivated by a need to be "engaged" by what she is working on, avoiding boredom by playing characters who possess more than one dimension. "I'm not interested in doing more films that are being made," she asserts. "There are so few beautifully written scripts that if there's something with any promise, you latch on to it."[5]

Although she is remarkably beautiful, beauty has little to do with Meryl's success as an actress. It is what she *does* with her beauty that is important. Her pale face, expressive eyes, and enigmatic smile present a range of contradictory emotions simultaneously. Poised fascinatingly between beauty and harshness, she is thoroughly a creature of change, her expression shadowed by a dazzlingly mutability, capable of an instant change in a state of emotion or mind.

Her physical and emotional mutability have enabled her to create memorable, unconventional roles that are singularly different from each other, so that typecasting has never been a threat to her career. As Joseph Papp once said: "I'm convinced we haven't yet begun to see the richness of her talent."[6] Meryl's unpredictability is an important element in her success. She has developed a reputation for a willingness to constantly test her talents and range as an actress, to try anything as long as it was a challenge, to take risks without being concerned that a particular role might damage her career.

Meryl's extraordinary instinct for the impromptu has earned her the respect of her peers in the theater, many of whom consider her to be the pure theatrical embodiment of the mysteries of creativity, giftedness and genius. They treat her like a queen in a profession fraught with jealousy and prima donnas. Joseph Papp adds: "Meryl cannot be compared with anyone. She stands very much alone. She is one of those pure actresses who has the capacity to inhabit her characters and make them seem real, not just pale imitations. You can see blood run through her characters."[7] Arvin Brown, her director at Yale's Long Wharf Theater, is another of her ardent admirers. "I think she is the major actress of her generation. Her external transformations trigger a much more profound inner change. Just as with Olivier, there is nothing she cannot do."[8]

Meryl's film directors and co-stars are equally effusive in describing what they consider her unique talent. They afford Meryl the respect usually reserved for actresses of the caliber of Katharine Hepburn and Bette Davis. Michael Cimino, who directed her in *The Deer Hunter*, considers Meryl "the dominant figure of the '80s."[9] Mike Nichols is utterly charmed by Meryl, adding: "Meryl's got to be one of those phenomena, like Garbo, that happens only once in a generation."[10] Even as demanding a co-star as Dustin Hoffman says: "She's going to be the Eleanor Roosevelt of acting."[11] Jerry Schatzberg, who directed Meryl in *The Seduction of Joe Tynan*, affirms: "She's going to be the next major American actress to be offered everything."[12]

But what does Meryl herself consider her greatest strength? "I'd like to think that people can sense the great appetite that I have for dramatizing things," she says. "I like peeling away the surface and presenting two sides of a person. Acting is my way of investigating human nature and having fun at the same time."[13] She considers herself an interpreter. "If actors are just reproducing an author's ideas, there would be no reason for critics reviewing different ways of presenting them."[14]

In interpreting her characters, Meryl has acquired the reputation among her colleagues as a perfectionist who demands a great deal of herself and her co-stars. As a totally dedicated artist, she can be aggressive in arguing for a realistic context in which to develop her character when she is convinced a script change is necessary to reveal the subtle complexities of her film persona. This trait is not the result of a self-centered egotism, but the aspirations of a gifted technician who ceaselessly strives to perfect her performances to make her characters' motivations ring true. Joseph Papp has long admired Meryl's professionally high standards regarding her work. "She is a very strong woman. When she fights for her point of view, there is none of the sweet, jolly, funloving Meryl, but she is also very giving. I never heard her put anyone down."[15]

Dustin Hoffman once made an important distinction in assessing Meryl's talent. He said, "Meryl stands not above very talented people but apart from them."[16] What sets her apart from her screen contemporaries is an intuitive knowledge of the contradictions of the human heart. Meryl calls it "ambiguity."[17] This is what she conveys in each of her characters, with the extraordinary ability to communicate all of them simultaneously. One of her colleagues states that "her greatest strength is in showing several emotions at once, the two or three or four feelings that tumble around in our heads in tandem."[18]

Meryl is completely immersed in the subtleties of her craft, constantly measuring herself against her own strict standards of excellence. "A movie is nothing until it comes to *be*," she insists. "It's really picked out of the air. Everything is full of fear and mystery. We're never quite sure what we have in the can, never quite sure what we're doing until we see what we've done. Then, at last, when we can actually *touch* it, that's thrilling!"[19] Joseph Papp has long been a fascinated observer of Meryl's dedication and strict self-discipline. "She's not unaware of her career, but her strongest commitment is to her acting. She's a shrewd analyst of herself. When she works, she tortures herself to reach the truth; that's her pain. She constantly has to plumb herself."[20]

Although she is the most sought-after actress on stage and screen, Meryl still gets nervous because her rise has been too swift, too easy. "I'm not really self-analytical," she says, "but I've been thinking that maybe a lot of my anxiety may have to do with . . . my own incredible good fortune. So much good fortune has come to me, and I think somewhere, somebody's got to pay."[21] She is aware that overnight successes often engender jealousy and resentment in the film industry, and a lot of criticism and backbiting. "I'm sure everybody's chomping at the bit to do that," she confesses. "It's because of all the glowing, gushy things that have been said."[22]

This anxiety is masked by the calm, self-assured perfectionist that audiences see on stage and screen. But those close to her have seen the torment she goes through in creating a character. Long-time friend Elizabeth Wilson remembers: "Though you don't see it when she's performing, Meryl suffers greatly before an opening. She perspires, she paces, I don't know if she actually gets sick, but she's very, very nervous — more so than almost anyone I've known."[23]

Meryl feels the stresses of her profession, but her means of coping with those stresses are firmly rooted in her concept of just plain common sense and in her art. "Why do people feel that you have to be neurotic to be an artist?" she scoffs. "I don't understand that concept. . . . If you feel anxious, if you feel you're losing your balance, you stop working. . . . I think no matter what you do, whether you're a housewife or have a career, you have to find a way of opting for a sanity break when you need it. Otherwise, you'll end up on a psychiatrist's couch."[24]

She can easily cope with the professional pressures; more difficult are the intrusions that fame brought into her privacy. Rarely does she discuss her personal life, which she views as peddling her intimacies. "It's so demeaning to discuss something that means a lot," she explains. "It takes a piece of me to talk about that — it's like selling it down the river. I hate being scrutinized . . . with people checking out my hair, my dress or whatever. I don't do well in these situations, but that's okay — because it has nothing to do with what I do. I chose acting because it happens to be my strong suit, but I challenge the right of the public to know me as a person. People assume that if you've done anything memorable, you should be stripped of your constitutional right to privacy."[25]

Meryl has always kept a strict division between her professional and private lives, and she refuses to insulate herself in the trappings of stardom. "I wouldn't like to be insulated against normal, everyday experiences, the vicissitudes, the problems. It's good to have all of those things and remain alive so that you have something to bring to each day."[26]

As a part of her desire not to lose touch with the real world, she is willing to forsake her privacy to venture into political and social protest, lending her support to nuclear disarmament and assistance to the disadvantaged.

As a result of her activism in nuclear disarmament, she received the Helen Caldicott Leadership Award from the Women's Action for Nuclear Disarmament (WAND) in 1984. "My commitment is quite emotional," she says. "Although I'm not completely comfortable standing on a platform speaking publicly, I'm also a mother and intimately involved in the next century. I want us to get there, and I have many fears we won't unless the tide of armaments is stopped."[27] Her award came through her participation in the Union of Concerned Scientists and the Performers' Action for Nuclear Disarmament, two organizations to which she has devoted countless hours of her time and talent.

Meryl has also done a great deal for more artistic freedom and participation for actresses in films. Because of her authorship of the courtroom scene in *Kramer vs. Kramer*, she paved the way for intelligent actresses to be not only acceptable, but desirable as well. Now many more actresses are involved in writing, producing and other creative input into films, and they credit Meryl for this achievement.

Although Meryl may now have her pick of the most desirable female leading roles in Hollywood and on the stage, she prefers character roles, and should she find that one day she is no longer offered leading parts, she will be content. "I have a view of my career and my craft as being an ongoing thing, and I have tried very hard not to believe any of my publicity, either good or bad, to put it out of my mind, understand the residual stuff is me. That's what is going to be here and I hope that is what is going to work, year after year, when I'm no longer on the cover of magazines."[28]

Perhaps that day will come, but it seems unlikely. Much more likely is the probability that her versatile talent will produce subtle nuances for a broad range of characters in memorable performances that will entertain audiences for generations to come. She has been described as being in her prime, but Alan Pakula has summed up the feelings of her fellow actors, directors and millions of fans: "She's going to have a *lot* of primes. In her eighties, Meryl Streep will be giving great performances."[29]

Filmography

The Deadliest Season (CBS, Titus Productions, 1977)
Executive Producer: Herbert Brodkin
Producer: Robert Berger
Director: Robert Markowitz
Teleplay: Ernest Kinoy
From the story by Ernest Kinoy, Tom King
Photography: Alan Metzger
Editor: Stephen A. Rotter
Music: Dick Hyman
Art Director: Richard Bianchi
Cast: Michael Moriarty (*Gerry Miller*), Kevin Conway (*George Graff*), Sully Boyar (*Tom Feeney*), Jill Eikenberry (*Carole Eskanazi*), Walter McGinn (*D.A. Horace Meade*), Meryl Streep (*Sharon Miller*), Andrew Duggan (*Al Miller*), Patrick O'Neal (*Bertram Fowler*), Paul D'Amato (*Dave Eskanazi*), Mason Adams (*Bill Cairns*), Mel Boudrot (*Coach Bryant*), Tom Quinn (*Trainer Doyle*), Ronald Weyand (*Judge Reinhardt*), Dino Narrizano (*Referee Merritt*), George Petrie (*President Mac-Cloud*), Eddie Moran (*Eddie Miller*), Frank Bongiorno (*Rene Beavois*), Rudy Hornish (*Waiter*), Alan North (*Detective Forscher*), Ian Sturart (*Jury Foreman*).
Running Time: 110 minutes

Julia (20th Century–Fox, 1977)
Producer: Richard Roth
Executive Producer: Julian Derode
Director: Fred Zinnemann
Screenplay: Alvin Sargent
Based on the book *Pentimento* by Lillian Hellman
Photography: Douglas Slocombe
Editor: Walter Murch
Music: Georges Delerue
Cast: Jane Fonda (*Lillian Hellman*), Vanessa Redgrave (*Julia*), Jason Robards (*Dashiell Hammett*), Maximilian Schell (*Johann*), Hal Holbrook (*Alan Campbell*), Rosemary Murphy (*Dorothy Parker*), Meryl Streep (*Anne Marie*), Dora Doll (*Train Passenger*), Elisabeth Mortensen (*Train Passenger*), John Glover (*Sammy*), Lisa Pelikan (*Young Julia*), Susan Jones (*Young Lillian*), Cathleen Nesbitt (*Grandmother*), Maurice Denham (*Undertaker*), Gerard Buhr (*Passport Officer*), Stefan Gryft ("*Hamlet*"), Phillip Siegel (*Little Boy*), Molly Urquhart (*Woman*), Antony Carrick (*Butler*), Ann Queensberry (*Woman in Berlin Station*), Edmond Bernard (*Man in Berlin Station*), Jacques David (*Fat Man*), Jacqueline Staup (*Woman in Green Hat*).
Running Time: 118 minutes

Holocaust (NBC, Titus Productions, 1978)
Executive Producer:Herbert Brodkin

127

Producer: Robert "Buzz" Berger
Director: Marvin J. Chomsky
Teleplay: Gerald Green
Photography: Brian West
Supervising Editor: Stephen A. Rotter
Music: Morton Gould
Art Directors: Jurgen Kiebach, Theo Harisch
Cast: Tom Bell (*Adolph Eichmann*), Joseph Bottoms (*Rudi Weiss*), Tovah Feldshuh (*Helena Slomova*), Marius Goring (*Herr Palitz*), Rosemary Harris (*Berta Weiss*), Anthony Haygarth (*Heinz Muller*), Ian Holm (*Heinrich Himmler*), Lee Montague (*Uncle Sasha*), Michael Moriarty (*Erik Dorf*), Deborah Norton (*Marta Dorf*), George Rose (*Lowy*), Robert Stephens (*Uncle Kurt Dorf*), Meryl Streep (*Inga Helms Weiss*), Sam Wanamaker (*Moses Weiss*), David Warner (*Reinhard Heydrick*), Fritz Weaver (*Josef Weiss*), James Woods (*Karl Weiss*), Sean Arnold (*Hoefle*), Fohn Baily (*Anna Weiss*), Kate Jaenicke (*Frau Lowy*), Charles Korvin (*Dr. Kohn*).
Running Time: 9½ hours

The Deer Hunter (Universal, 1978)
Producers: Barry Spikings, Michael Deeley, Michael Cimino, John Peverall
Director: Michael Cimino
Screenplay: Deric Washburn
Story: Deric Washburn, Michael Cimino, Louis Garfinkle, Quinn K. Redeker
Photography: Vilmos Zsigmond
Art Directors: Ron Hobbs, Kim Swados
Editor: Peter Zinner
Music: Stanley Myers
Cast: Robert De Niro (*Michael*), John Cazale (*Stan*), John Savage (*Steven*), Christopher Walken (*Nick*), Meryl Streep (*Linda*), George Dzundza (*John*), Chuck Aspegren (*Axel*), Shirley Stoler (*Steven's Mother*), Rutanya Alda (*Angela*), Pierre Segui (*Julien*), Mady Kaplan (*Axel's Girl*), Amy Wright (*Bridesmaid*), Mary Ann Haenel (*Stan's Girl*), Richard Kuss (*Linda's Father*), Joe Grifasi (*Bandleader*), Christopher Colomib, Jr. (*Wedding Man*), Victoria Karnafel (*Sad Looking Girl*), Jack Scardino (*Cold Old Man*), Joe Strand (*Bingo Caller*), Henen Tomko (*Helen*), Paul D'Amato (*Sargeant*).
Running Time: 183 minutes

The Seduction of Joe Tynan (Universal, 1979)
Producer: Martin Bregman
Executive Producer: Louis A. Stroller
Director: Jerry Shatzberg
Screenplay: Alan Alda
Photography: Adam Holender
Editor: Evan Lottman
Art Director: David Chapman
Music: Bill Conti
Assistant Directors: Ralph Singleton, Udi Bennett
Cast: Alan Alda (*Joe Tynan*), Barbara Harris (*Ellie*), Meryl Streep (*Karen Traynor*), Rip Torn (*Senator Kittner*), Melvyn Douglas (*Senator Birney*), Charles Kimbrough (*Francis*), Carrie Nye (*Aldena Kittner*), Michael Higgins (*Senator Pardew*), Blanche Baker (*Janet*), Maureen Anderman (*Joe's Secretary*), Chris Arnold (*Jerry*), John Badila (*Reporter on TV*), Robert Christian (*Arthur Briggs*), Maurice Copeland (*Edward Anderson*), Lu Elrod (*Congresswoman at Party*), Clarence

Felder (*Golf Pro*), Gus Fleming (*Eric*), Merv Griffin (*Himself*), Marian Hailey-Moss (*Sheila Lerner*), Dan Hedaya (*Alex Heller*), Bill Moor (*Barry Traynor*).
Running Time: 107 minutes

Manhattan (United Artists, 1979)
Producer: Charles H. Joffe
Executive Producer: Robert Greenhut
Director: Woody Allen
Screenplay: Woody Allen, Marshall Brickman
Photography: Gordon Willis
Editor: Susan E. Morse
Music: George Gershwin
Assistant Directors: Fredric B. Blankfein, Joan Spiegel Feinstein
Cast: Woody Allen (*Issac Davis*), Diane Keaton (*Mary Wilke*), Michael Murphy (*Yale*), Mariel Hemingway (*Tracy*), Meryl Streep (*Jill*), Anne Byrne (*Emily*), Karen Ludwig (*Connie*), Michael O'Donoghue (*Dennis*), Victor Truro (*Party Guest*), Tisa Farrow (*Party Guest*), Helen Hanft (*Party Guest*), Bella Abzug (*Guest of Honor*), Gary Weis (*Television Director*), Kenny Vance (*Television Producer*), Charles Levin (*Television Actor*), Karen Allen (*Television Actor*), David Rasche (*Television Actor*), Damion Sheller (*Issac's son, Willie*), Wallace Shawn (*Jeremiah*).
Running Time: 96 minutes

Kramer vs. Kramer (Columbia Pictures, 1979)
Producer: Stanley R. Jaffe
Director: Robert Benton
Screenplay: Robert Benton
Based on the novel by Avery Corman
Director of Photography: Nestor Almendros, A.S.C.
Film Editor: Jerry Greenberg
Music: Henry Purcell
Cast: Dustin Hoffman (*Ted Kramer*), Meryl Streep (*Joanna Kramer*), Jane Alexander (*Margaret Phelps*), Justin Henry (*Billy Kramer*), Howard Duff (*John Shaunessy*), George Coe (*Jim O'Connor*), JoBeth Williams (*Phyllis Bernard*), Bill Moor (*Gressen*).
Running Time: 105 minutes

The French Lieutenant's Woman (United Artists, 1981)
Producer: Leon Clore
Director: Karel Reisz
Screenplay: Harold Pinter
Based on the novel by John Fowles
Photography: Freddie Francis
Editor: John Bloom
Music: Carl Davis
Cast: Meryl Streep (*Sarah/Anna*), Jeremy Irons (*Charles/Mike*), Hilton McRae (*Sam*), Emily Morgan (*Mary*), Charlotte Mitchell (*Mrs. Tranter*), Lynsey Baxter (*Ernestina*), Jean Faulds (*Cook*), Peter Vaughan (*Mr. Freeman*), Colin Jeavons (*Vicar*), Liz Smith (*Mrs. Fairley*), Patience Collier (*Mrs. Poulteney*), John Barrett (*Dairyman*), Leo McKern (*Dr. Grogan*), Arabella Weir (*Girl on Undercliff*), Ben Forster (*Boy on Undercliff*), Catherine Willmer (*Dr. Grogan's Housekeeper*).
Running time: 117 minutes

Sophie's Choice (Universal, 1982)
    Producers: Alan J. Pakula, Keith Barish
    Director: Alan J. Pakula
    Screenplay: Alan J. Pakula
    Based on the novel by William Styron
    Photography: Nestor Almendros, A.S.C.
    Editor: Evan Lottman
    Original Music: Marvin Hamlisch
    Cast: Meryl Streep (*Sophie*), Kevin Kline (*Nathan*), Peter MacNicol (*Stingo*), Josef Sommer (*Narrator*), Rita Karin (*Yetta*), Stephen D. Newman (*Larry*), Greta Turken (*Leslie Lapidus*), Josh Mostel (*Morris Fink*), Marcell Rosenblatt (*Astrid Weinstein*), Moishe Rosenfeld (*Moise Rosenblum*), Robin Bartlett (*Lillian Grossman*), Eugene Lipinski (*Polish Professor*), Hohn Rothman (*Librarian*), Joseph Leon (*Dr. Blackstock*), David Wohl (*English Teacher*), Nina Polan (*English Student*), Alexander Sirotin (*English Student*), Joseph Tobin (*Reporter*), Cortez Nance (*Bellboy*), Gunther Maria Halmer (*Rudolf Hoess*), Karlheinz Hackl (*SS Doctor*), Ulli Fessl (*Frau Hoess*), Melanie Pianka (*Emmi Hoess*), Krystyna Karkowska (*Prisoner Housekeeper*), Katharina Thalbach (*Wanda*), Neddim Prohic (*Josef*), Jennifer Lawn (*Sophie's daughter*), Adrian Kalitka (*Sophie's son*), Peter Wegenbreth (*Hoess' Aide*), Vida Jerman (*Female SS Guard*), Ivo Pajer (*Sophie's Father*), Michaela Karacic (*Sophie as a child*).
    Running Time: 157 minutes

Still of the Night (MGM-UA, 1982)
    Producer: Arlene Donovan
    Director: Robert Benton
    Screenplay: Robert Benton
    Story: David Newman, Robert Benton
    Associate Producers: Wolfgang Glattes, Kenneth Utt
    Photography: Nestor Almendros, A.S.C.
    Editor: Jerry Greenberg
    Music: John Kander
    Cast: Roy Scheider (*Sam Rice*), Meryl Streep (*Brooke Reynolds*), Jessica Tandy (*Grace Rice*), Joe Grifasi (*Joseph Vicucci*), Sara Botsford (*Gail Phillips*), Josef Sommers (*George Bynum*), Rikke Borge (*Heather Wilson*), Irving Metzman (*Murray Gordon*), Larry Joshua (*Mugger*), Tom Norton (*Auctioneer*), Richmond Hoxie (*Mr. Harris*), Hyon Cho (*Mr. Chang*), Danielle Cusson (*Girl*), John Bentley (*Nightwatchman*), George A. Tooks (*Elevator Operator*), Sigrunn Omark (*Receptionist*), Randy Jurgenson (*Car Thief*).
    Running Time: 91 minutes

Silkwood (20th Century–Fox, 1983)
    Producers: Mike Nichols, Michael Hausman
    Director: Mike Nichols
    Screenplay: Nora Ephron, Alice Arlen
    Music: Georges Delerue
    Executive Producers: Buzz Hirsch, Larry Cano
    Editor: Sam O'Steen
    Photography: Miroslav Onricek
    Cast: Meryl Streep (*Karen Silkwood*), Kurt Russell (*Drew Stephens*), Cher (*Dolly Pelliker*), Craig T. Nelson (*Winston*), Diana Scarwid (*Angela*), Fred Ward (*Morgan*), Ron Silver (*Paul Stone*), Charles Hallahan (*Earl Lapin*), Josef Sommer (*Max Richter*), Sudie Bond (*Thelma*), Henderson Forsythe (*Quincy Bissell*), E.

Katherine Kerr (*Gilda Schultz*), David Straithairn (*Mace Hurley*), J.C. Quinn (*Curtis Schultz*), Kent Broadhurst (*Carl*), Richard Hamilton (*Georgie*), Les Lannom (*Jimmy*), M. Emmet Walsh (*Walt Yarbourgh*), Graham Jarvis (*Union Meeting Doctor*).
Running Time: 131 minutes

Falling in Love (Paramount Pictures, 1984)
Producer: Marvin Worth
Director: Ulu Grosbard
Screenplay: Michael Cristofer
Director of Photography: Peter Suschitzky
Film Editor: Michael Kahn
Music: Dave Grusin
Cast: Meryl Streep (*Molly Gilmore*), Robert De Niro (*Frank Raftis*), Harvey Keitel (*Ed Lasky*), Jane Kaczmarek (*Ann Raftis*), George Martin (*John Trainer*), David Clennon (*Brian Gilmore*), Dianne Wiest (*Isabelle*), Victor Argo (*Victor Rawlins*), Wiley Earl (*Mike Raftis*), Jesse Bradford (*Joe Raftis*).
Running Time: 106 minutes

Plenty (20th Century–Fox, 1985)
Director: Fred Schepisi
Producers: Edward R. Pressman, Joseph Papp
Screenplay: David Hare; based on his play of the same title
Photography: Ian Baker
Music: Bruce Smeaton
Editor: Peter Honess
Cast: Meryl Streep (*Susan*), Charles Dance (*Raymond Brock*), Sam Neill (*Lazar*), John Geilgud (*Sir Leonard Darwin*), Ian McKellen (*Sir Andrew Charleson*), Tracey Ullman (*Alice*), Sting (*Mick*), Andre Maranne (*Villon*), Tristram Jellinek (*Dauncey*), Ian Wallace (*Medlicott*), Andy De La Tour (*Randall*).
Running Time: 124 minutes.

Out of Africa (Universal, 1985)
Producer: Sydney Pollack
Director: Sydney Pollack
Screenplay: Kurt Luedtke, based on "Out of Africa" and other writings by Isak Dinesen
Photography: David Watkin
Editors: Fredric Steinkamp, William Steinkamp, Pembroke Herring, Sheldon Kahn
Music: John Barry
Cast: Meryl Streep (*Karen*), Robert Redford (*Denys*), Klaus Maria Brandauer (*Bror*), Michael Kitchen (*Berkeley*), Malick Bowens (*Farah*), Joseph Thaiaka (*Kamante*), Stephen Kinyanjui (*Kinanjui*), Michael Gough (*Delamere*), Suzanna Hamilton (*Felicity*), Rachel Kempson (*Lady Belfield*), Graham Crowden (*Lord Belfield*), Leslie Phillips (*Sir Joseph*), Shane Rimmer (*Belknap*), Mike Bugara (*Juma*).
Running Time: 150 minutes

Heartburn (Paramount, 1986)
Producers: Mike Nichols, Robert Greenhut
Director: Mike Nichols
Screenplay: Nora Ephron, based on her novel

Photography: Nestor Almendros
Editor: Sam O'Steen
Music: Carly Simon
Cast: Meryl Streep (*Rachel*), Jack Nicholson (*Mark*), Jeff Daniels (*Richard*), Maureen Stapleton (*Vera*), Stockard Channing (*Julie*), Richard Masur (*Arthur*), Catherine O'Hara (*Betty*), Steven Hill (*Harry*), Milos Forman (*Dmitri*), Natalie Stern (*Annie*), Karen Akers (*Thelma*), Aida Linares (*Juanita*), Anna Maria Horsford (*Della*).

Notes

1. Images

1. "Spotlight: Close-Up," *Seventeen*, Feb. 1977, p. 64.

2. In the Beginning

1. Jack Kroll, "A Star for the '80's," *Newsweek*, Jan. 7, 1980, p. 56.
2. Diane de Dubovay, "Meryl Streep," *Ladies' Home Journal*, March 1980, p. 39.
3. de Dubovay, "Meryl Streep," p. 39.
4. Paul Gray, "A Mother Finds Herself," *Time*, Dec. 3, 1979, p. 81.
5. de Dubovay, "Meryl Streep," p. 39.
6. de Dubovay, "Meryl Streep," p. 40.
7. John Skow, "What Makes Meryl Magic," *Time*, Sept. 7, 1981, p. 41.
8. Gray, "A Mother Finds Herself," p. 41.
9. "Spotlight: Close-Up," p. 64.
10. Susan Dworkin, "Meryl Streep to the Rescue!" *Ms.*, Feb. 1979, p. 88.
11. David Rosenthal, "Meryl Streep: Stepping In and Out of Roles," *Rolling Stone*, Oct. 15, 1981, p. 66.
12. Jane Hall, "From Homecoming Queen to 'Holocaust': Actress Meryl Streep," *T.V. Guide*, June 24, 1978, p. 14.
13. de Dubovay, "Meryl Streep," p. 40.
14. Gray, "A Mother Finds Herself," p. 81.
15. Rosenthal, "Meryl Streep: Stepping In and Out of Roles," p. 67.
16. Mel Gussow, "The Rising Star of Meryl Streep," *New York Times Magazine*, Feb. 14, 1979, p. 24.
17. Dworkin, "Meryl Streep to the Rescue!" p. 88.
18. Gussow, "The Rising Star of Meryl Streep," p. 24.
19. Dworkin, "Meryl Streep to the Rescue!" p. 88.

3. The Making of a Legend

1. Kroll, "A Star for the '80's," p. 55.
2. "Spotlight: Close-Up," p. 64.
3. Gray, "A Mother Finds Herself," p. 81.
4. Gussow, "The Rising Star of Meryl Streep," p. 24.
5. Gussow, "The Rising Star of Meryl Streep," p. 24.
6. Rosenthal, "Meryl Streep: Stepping In and Out of Roles," p. 67.
7. Dworkin, "Meryl Streep to the Rescue!" p.88
8. Dworkin, "Meryl Streep to the Rescue!" p.88
9. Gussow, "The Rising Star of Meryl Streep," p. 24.

10. Rosenthal, "Meryl Streep: Stepping In and Out of Roles," p. 67.
11. Kroll, "A Star for the '80's," p. 55.
12. Skow, "What Makes Meryl Magic," p. 41.
13. Skow, "What Makes Meryl Magic," p. 41.
14. Kroll, "A Star for the '80's," p. 55.

4. The Crucible

1. Tony Scherman, "'Holocaust' Survivor Shoots 'Deer Hunter,' Shuns Fame," *Feature*, Feb. 1979, p. 14.
2. Gussow, "The Rising Star of Meryl Streep," p. 41.
3. Dworkin, "Meryl Streep to the Rescue!" p. 88.
4. Dworkin, "Meryl Streep to the Rescue!" p. 88.
5. Dworkin, "Meryl Streep to the Rescue!" p. 88.
6. Skow, "What Makes Meryl Magic," p. 47.
7. Kroll, "A Star for the '80's," pp. 55–56.
8. Judy Klemesrud, "From Yale Drama to 'Fanatic Nun,'" *New York Times*, August 18, 1976, III, p. 1.

5. Love—and Tragedy

1. Thomas Lask, "Rudd, Meryl Streep, Actors to Hilt," *New York Times*, June 14, 1976, III, p. 1.
2. Lask, "Rudd, Meryl Streep, Actors to Hilt," p. 1.
3. Dworkin, "Meryl Streep to the Rescue!" p. 48
4. Lask, "Rudd, Meryl Streep, Actors to Hilt," p. 1.
5. Martine Latour, "Interview: Meryl Streep on Julia," *Mademoiselle*, March 1977, p. 76.
6. "Spotlight: Close-Up," p. 64.
7. Latour, "Interview: Meryl Streep on Julia," p. 76.
8. Latour, "Interview: Meryl Streep on Julia," p. 76.
9. Latour, "Interview: Meryl Streep on Julia," p. 76.
10. Joan Juliet Buck, "Meryl Streep: More of a Woman," *Vogue*, June 1980, p. 226.
11. Dworkin, "Meryl Streep to the Rescue!" p. 86.
12. Scot Haller, "Star Treks," *Horizon*, August 1978, p. 47.
13. Gussow, "The Rising Star of Meryl Streep," p. 24.

6. Conundrum

1. Dworkin, "Meryl Streep to the Rescue!" p. 49.
2. Hall, "From Homecoming Queen to 'Holocaust': Actress Meryl Streep," p. 15.
3. Gray, "A Mother Finds Herself," p. 81.
4. Gussow, "The Rising Star of Meryl Streep," p. 26.
5. Gray, "A Mother Finds Herself," p. 81.
6. Gussow, "A Mother Finds Herself," p. 26.
7. Kroll, "A Star for the '80's," p. 56.
8. Kroll, "A Star for the '80's," p. 56.
9. Dworkin, "Meryl Streep to the Rescue!" p. 49.
10. Haller, "Star Treks," p. 47.
11. Dworkin, "Meryl Streep to the Rescue!" p. 48.

12. Haller, "Star Treks," p. 47.
13. Gussow, "The Rising Star of Meryl Streep," p. 26.

7. *Resurrection*

1. de Dubovay, "Meryl Streep," p. 36.
2. de Dubovay, "Meryl Streep," p. 36.
3. Kroll, "A Star for the '80's," p. 56.
4. Elaine Dutka, "Talking with Meryl Streep," *Redbook*, Sept. 1982, p. 14.
5. de Dubovay, "Meryl Streep," p. 196.
6. Stephen M. Silverman, "Life Without Mother," *American Film*, August 1979, p. 54.
7. Jack Kroll, "A Star for the '80's," p. 56.
8. Gray, "A Mother Finds Herself," p. 80.
9. Gray, "A Mother Finds Herself," p. 80.
10. Gray, "A Mother Finds Herself," p. 80.
11. Kroll, "A Star for the '80's," p. 56.
12. Scherman, "'Holocaust' Survivor Shoots 'Deer Hunter,' Shuns Fame," p. 14.
13. Gussow, "The Rising Star of Meryl Streep," p. 26.

8. *Reluctant Star*

1. Skow, "What Makes Meryl Magic," p.41.
2. Dutka, "Talking with Meryl Streep," p. 14.
3. de Dubovay, "Meryl Streep," p. 36.
4. Scherman, "'Holocaust' Survivor Shoots 'Deer Hunter,' Shuns Fame," p. 13.
5. Gussow, "The Rising Star of Meryl Streep," p. 26.
6. Gussow, "The Rising Star of Meryl Streep," p. 26.
7. de Dubovay, "Meryl Streep," p. 40.
8. "Meryl Streep: Hollywood Finds a Refreshing '79-Style Golden Girl Who Insists on Being Her Own Woman," *People Weekly*, December 24, 1979, p. 76.
9. David Denby, "Movies: Meryl Streep Is Madonna and Siren as the French Lieutenant's Woman," *New York*, Sept. 21, 1981, p. 27.
10. Denby, "Movies," p. 27.
11. Bob Greene, "Streep," *Esquire*, Dec. 1984, p. 440.

9. *The Year of Streep*

1. "The Crossed Fingers Worked, but Then Meryl Left Her Oscar in the John," *People Weekly*, April 28, 1980, p. 32.
2. Mason Wiley and Damien Bona, *Inside Oscar: The Unofficial History of the Academy Awards*, Ballantine Books, New York, New York, 1986, p. 579.
3. "The Crossed Fingers Worked, but Then Meryl Left Her Oscar in the John," p. 32.
4. Buck, "Meryl Streep: More of a Woman," p. 144.
5. Skow, "What Makes Meryl Magic," p. 47.
6. Mel Gussow, "A Stormy Courtship," *Horizon*, Oct. 1981, p. 41.
7. Skow, "What Makes Meryl Magic," p. 47.
8. Gussow, "A Stormy Courtship," p. 40.

9. Gussow, "A Stormy Courtship," p. 41.
10. Skow, "What Makes Meryl Magic," p. 40.
11. Gussow, "A Stormy Courtship," p. 41.
12. Gussow, "A Stormy Courtship," p. 41.
13. Gussow, "A Stormy Courtship," p. 41.
14. Dutka, "Talking with Meryl Streep," p. 14.
15. Skow, "What Makes Meryl Magic," p. 47.
16. Dutka, "Talking with Meryl Streep," p. 12.
17. Dutka, "Talking with Meryl Streep," p. 12.
18. Dutka, "Talking with Meryl Streep," p. 12.
19. Dutka, "Talking with Meryl Streep," p. 14.

10. Winning It All

1. Aljean Harmetz, "Miss Streep and Kline Cast in Movie 'Sophie,'" *New York Times*, July 22, 1982, III, p. 21.
2. Harmetz, "Miss Streep and Kline Cast in Movie 'Sophie,'" p. 21.
3. Harmetz, "Miss Streep and Kline Cast in Movie 'Sophie,'" p. 21.
4. Harmetz, "Miss Streep and Kline Cast in Movie 'Sophie,'" p. 21.
5. Harmetz, "Miss Streep and Kline Cast in Movie 'Sophie,'" p. 21.
6. John Culhane, "Pakula's Approach," *New York Times Magazine*, November 21, 1982, VI, p. 64.
7. Natalie Gittleson, "Meryl Streep: Surprising Superstar," *McCall's*, March 1983, p. 36.
8. Denby, "Movies," p. 26
9. Gittleson, "Meryl Streep: Surprising Superstar," p. 36.
10. Gittleson, "Meryl Streep: Surprising Superstar," p. 36.
11. Gittleson, "Meryl Streep: Surprising Superstar," p. 38.
12. Gittleson, "Meryl Streep: Surprising Superstar," p. 38.
13. Culhane, "Pakula's Approach," p. 66.
14. Culhane, "Pakula's Approach," p. 140.
15. Dutka, "Talking with Meryl Streep," p. 12.
16. Gittleson, "Meryl Streep: Surprising Superstar," p. 38.
17. Gittleson, "Meryl Streep: Surprising Superstar," p. 38.
18. Dutka, "Talking with Meryl Streep," p. 12.
19. Gittleson, "Meryl Streep: Surprising Superstar," p. 36.
20. Gittleson, "Meryl Streep: Surprising Superstar," p. 38.
21. Dutka, "Talking with Meryl Streep," p. 13.
22. Gittleson, "Meryl Streep: Surprising Superstar," p. 38.
23. Gittleson, "Meryl Streep: Surprising Superstar," p. 38.
24. Lena Williams, "Miss Streep Urges Class of '83 to Try for Excellence," *New York Times*, May 23, 1983, II, p. 2.
25. Williams, "Miss Streep Urges Class of '83 to Try for Excellence," p. 2.
26. Williams, "Miss Streep Urges Class of '83 to Try for Excellence," p. 2.
27. Dorothy J. Gatter, "City U. Students Urged to Higher Goal," *New York Times*, June 3, 1983, II, p. 3.

11. Silkwood

1. "In Search of 'Silkwood,'" *American Film*, Dec. 1983, p. 52
2. "In Search of 'Silkwood,'" p. 52

3. "In Search of 'Silkwood,'" p. 52.
4. "In Serach of 'Silkwood,'" p. 53.
5. "In Search of 'Silkwood,'" p. 53.
6. Jim Jerome, "Cher Finds a New Life," *People Weekly*, Jan. 23, 1984, p. 82.
7. Jerome, "Cher Finds a New Life," p. 82.
8. Jerome, "Cher Finds a New Life," p. 85.
9. Jerome, "Cher Finds a New Life," p. 85.
10. Jerome, "Cher Finds a New Life," p. 85.
11. Jerome, "Cher Finds a New Life," p. 85.
12. "Meryl Streep: Why I've Taken a Year Off for Motherhood," p. 154.
13. Jerome, "Cher Finds a New Life," p. 85.
14. "Meryl Streep: Why I've Taken a Year Off for Motherhood," p. 154.
15. "Meryl Streep: Why I've Taken a Year Off for Motherhood," p. 154.
16. Peter Carlson and Linda Witt, "*Silkwood's* Real-Life Characters Find Much to Praise — and a Few Inaccuracies — in the Hit Film," *People Weekly*, Feb. 20, 1984, p. 78.
17. Carlson and Witt, "*Silkwood's* Real-Life Characters Find Much to Praise — and a Few Inaccuracies — in the Hit Film," p. 77.
18. Carlson and Witt, "*Silkwood's* Real-Life Characters Find Much to Praise — and a Few Inaccuracies — in the Hit Film," p. 77.
19. Carlson and Witt, "*Silkwood's* Real-Life Characters Find Much to Praise — and a Few Inaccuracies — in the Hit Film," p. 81.
20. Wiley and Bona, *Inside Oscar*, p. 632.
21. Wiley and Bona, *Inside Oscar*, p. 632.

12. *Magic Meryl*

1. Gittleson, "Meryl Streep: Surprising Superstar," p. 38.
2. "Meryl Streep: Why I've Taken a Year Off for Motherhood," p. 153.
3. "Meryl Streep: Why I've Taken a Year Off for Motherhood," p. 153.
4. "Meryl Streep: Why I've Taken a Year Off for Motherhood," p. 153.
5. "Meryl Streep: Why I've Taken a Year Off for Motherhood," p. 153.
6. "Meryl Streep: Why I've Taken a Year Off for Motherhood," p. 153.
7. "Meryl Streep: Why I've Taken a Year Off for Motherhood," p. 154.
8. "Meryl Streep: Why I've Taken a Year Off for Motherhood," p. 154.
9. Glenn Collins, "Love Makes a Movie Comeback," *New York Times*, November 25, 1984, II, p. 1.
10. Collins, "Love Makes a Movie Comeback," p. 1.
11. Collins, "Love Makes a Movie Comeback," p. 28.
12. Collins, "Love Makes a Movie Comeback," p. 28.
13. Collins, "Love Makes a Movie Comeback," p. 28.
14. Collins, "Love Makes a Movie Comeback," p. 28.
15. Collins, "Love Makes a Movie Comeback," p. 28.
16. Collins, "Love Makes a Movie Comeback," p. 28.
17. "Entertainment Tonight," NBC-TV, October 17, 1985.
18. "Entertainment Tonight," NBC-TV, October 17, 1985.
19. "Entertainment Tonight," NBC-TV, October 17, 1985.
20. "Entertainment Tonight," NBC-TV, October 17, 1985.
21. "Entertainment Tonight," NBC-TV, October 17, 1985.
22. "Carol Wallace, "Scene: Streep and Redford Battle Lions, Snakes, Storms and Controversy to Bring *Out of Africa* to the Screen," *People*, Jan. 20, 1986, p. 89.

23. Wallace, "Scene," p. 89.
24. Wallace, "Scene," p. 89.
25. Wallace, "Scene," p. 90.
26. Wallace, "Scene," p. 90.
27. Wallace, "Scene," p. 90.
28. Wallace, "Scene," p. 97.
29. Jeff Rovin, "Thoroughly Modern Meryl," *Ladies' Home Journal*, August 1986, p. 151.
30. Rovin, "Thoroughly Modern Meryl," p. 152.
31. Rovin, "Thoroughly Modern Meryl," p. 154.
32. Rovin, "Thoroughly Modern Meryl," pp. 153–154.
33. Rovin, "Thoroughly Modern Meryl," p. 154.
34. Rovin, "Thoroughly Modern Meryl," p. 154.

13. Chameleon

1. Rosenthal, "Magic Streep: Stepping In and Out of Roles," p. 17.
2. Skow, "What Makes Meryl Magic," p. 38.
3. Rosenthal, "Meryl Streep: Stepping In and Out of Roles," p. 19.
4. Rosenthal, "Meryl Streep: Stepping In and Out of Roles," p. 19.
5. Rosenthal, "Meryl Streep: Stepping In and Out of Roles," p. 66.
6. Gussow, "The Rising Star of Meryl Streep," p. 24.
7. de Dubovay, "Meryl Streep," p. 36.
8. Gussow, "The Rising Star of Meryl Streep," p. 23; Kroll, "What Makes Meryl Magic," p. 40.
9. Dutka, "Meryl Streep: More of a Woman," p. 143.
10. Gittleson, "Meryl Streep: Surprising Superstar," p. 34.
11. Kroll, "A Star for the '80's," p. 56.
12. Gussow, "The Rising Star of Meryl Streep," p. 27.
13. Dutka, "Talking with Meryl Streep," p. 12.
14. Gussow, "The Rising Star of Meryl Streep," p. 28.
15. Gussow, "The Rising Star of Meryl Streep," p. 27.
16. Kroll, "Meryl Streep: Reluctant Superstar," p. 137.
17. Gittleson, "Meryl Streep: Surprising Superstar," p. 38.
18. Gittleson, "Meryl Streep: Surprising Superstar," p. 38.
19. Gittleson, "Meryl Streep: Surprising Superstar," p. 36.
20. Gussow, "The Rising Star of Meryl Streep," p. 27.
21. Rosenthal, "Meryl Streep: Stepping In and Out of Roles," p. 17.
22. Rosenthal, "Meryl Streep: Stepping In and Out of Roles," p. 17.
23. Rosenthal, "Meryl Streep: Stepping In and Out of Roles," p. 17.
24. de Dubovay, "Meryl Streep," p. 36.
25. Rosenthal, "Meryl Streep: Stepping In and Out of Roles," p. 66; Dutka, "Talking with Meryl Streep," pp. 12–14.
26. Buck, "Meryl Streep: More of a Woman," p. 226.
27. Kroll, "Meryl Streep: Reluctant Superstar," p. 196.
28. Buck, "Meryl Streep: More of a Woman," p. 226.
29. Gittleson, "Meryl Streep: Surprising Superstar," p. 38.

Bibliography

Bennetts, Leslie. "Kevin Kline's Great Leap to Filmdom." *New York Times*, II, p. 1, December 12, 1982.

Carlson, Peter, and Linda Witt. "Screen: Silkwood's Real-Life Characters Find Much to Praise—And a Few Inaccuracies—In the Hit Film." *People*, February 20, 1984, pp. 74–82.

"Close Up." *Seventeen*, February 1977, p. 64.

Collins, Glenn. "Love Makes a Movie Comeback." *New York Times*, November 25, 1984, II, p. 1.

"The Crossed Fingers Worked, but Then Meryl Left Her Oscar in the John." *People*, April 8, 1980, p. 3.

Culhane, John. "Pakula's Approach." *New York Times Magazine*, November 21, 1982, IV, pp. 64–66+.

de Dubovay, Diane. "Meryl Streep." *Ladies' Home Journal*, March 1980, p. 344.

Denby, David. "Movies." *New York*, September 21, 1981, pp. 26–7.

Dreifus, Claudia. "Meryl Streep: Why I've Taken a Year Off for Motherhood." *Ladies' Home Journal*, April 1984, pp. 48–9.

Dutka, Elaine. "Talking with Meryl Streep." *Redbook*, September 1982, pp. 12–14.

Dworkin, Susan. "Meryl Streep to the Rescue." *Ms.*, February 1979, pp. 47–5+

Gaiter, Dorothy J. "City U. Students Urged to Higher Goal." *New York Times*, June 3, 1983, II, p. 3.

Gittelson, Natalie. "Meryl Streep: Surprising Superstar." *McCall's*, March 1983, p. 34+.

Gray, Paul. "A Mother Finds Herself: The Silent Suffering of Meryl Streep." *Time*, December 3, 1979, pp. 80–81.

Greene, Bob. "Streep." *Esquire*, December 1984, pp. 441–443.

Gussow, Mel. "A Stormy Courtship." *Horizon*, August 1978, pp. 42–7.

Hall, Jane. "From Homecoming Queen to 'Holocaust,'" *T.V. Guide*, June 4, 1978, pp. 14–15.

Haller, Scot. "Star Treks." *Horizon*, August 1978, pp. 42–7.

Harmetz, Aljean. "Miss Streep and Kline Cast in Movie 'Sophie.' *New York Times*, July 22, 1981, III, p. 21.

"Hollywood Finds a Refreshing '79-Style Golden Girl Who Insists on Being Her Own Woman." *People*, December 24, 1979, p. 276.

Jerome, Jim. "Cher Finds a New Life." *People*, January 23, 1984, pp. 82–3+.

Kennedy, Harlan. "The Czech Director's Woman." *Film Comment*, September/October, 1981, p. 26–31.

Klemsrud, Judy. "From Yale Drama to 'Fanatic Nun.'" *New York Times*, August 13, 1976, III, p. 2.

Kroll, Jack. "Meryl Streep: Reluctant Superstar." *Ladies' Home Journal*, May 1985, pp. 137+.

_____. "A Star for the '80's." *Newsweek*, January 7, 1980, pp. 25–6.

Latour, Martine. "Meryl Streep on Julia." *Mademoiselle*, March 1977, p. 276.

Lindsey, Robert. "Stars Gird for Their Big Night." *New York Times*, April 15, 1980, II, p. 27.

"Notes on People." *New York Times*, January 5, 1980, p. 24.

"Notes on People." *New York Times*, April 9, 1980, II, p. 27.

Rich, Frank. "Grownups, Child, a Divorce, and Tears." *Time*, December 3, 1979, pp. 74–77.

Rosenthal, David. "Meryl Streep: Stepping In and Out of Roles." *Rolling Stone*, October 15, 1981, pp. 17–19+.

Rovin, Jeff. "Thoroughly Modern Meryl." *Ladies' Home Journal*, August 1986, pp. 100+.

Scherman, Tony. "'Holocaust' Survivor Shoots 'Deer Hunter,' Shuns Fame." *Feature*, February 1979, pp. 13–14.

Bibliography 141

Skrow, John. "What Makes Meryl Magic?" *Time*, September 7, 1981, pp. 38–47+.

Silverman, Stephen. "Life Without Mother." *American Film*, July–August, 1979, pp. 50–55.

Theatre World, 1974–1975, 1975–1976, 1976–1977, 1978–1979, 1980–1981.

Wallace, Carol. "Scene: Streep and Redford Battle Lions, Snakes, Storms and Controversy to Bring *Out of Africa* to the Screen." *People*, January 20, 1986, pp. 89–90+.

Watson, Linda E. "Amazing Meryl Streep," *Teen*, January 1980, pp. 23–4.

Williams, Lena. "Miss Streep Urges Class of '83 to Try for Excellence." *New York Times*, May 23, 1983.

Willis, John. *John Willis' Screen World*. 1978, 1979, 1980, 1981, 1983, 1984.

Index

143